At the Heart of Progress

Coal, Iron, and Steam since 1750

AT THE HEART *of* PROGRESS

COAL, IRON, AND STEAM SINCE 1750

Industrial Imagery from THE JOHN P. ECKBLAD COLLECTION

ACKLAND ART MUSEUM | THE UNIVERSITY OF NORTH CAROLINA AT CHAPEL HILL

Published 2009
Printed in the United States of America

This catalogue is published in conjunction with the exhibition
At the Heart of Progress: Coal, Iron, and Steam since 1750
Industrial Imagery from The Collection of John P. Eckblad,
presented by the Ackland Art Museum from January 24 – May 17, 2009.

ISBN: 978-0-8078-5980-3

Library of Congress Control Number: 2008944259

Designed by
The Splinter Group
Carrboro, North Carolina, USA

Printed by
Classic Graphics
Morrisville, North Carolina, USA

Distributed by
The University of North Carolina Press
www.uncpress.com

This publication is made possible by the William Hayes Ackland Trust and friends and members of the Ackland Art Museum.

From the Director

With an innate curiosity, a discerning eye, and the long-standing commitment of time and resources, John P. Eckblad has built an outstanding private collection of prints that help illuminate the impact of industry on the European and American landscape. The prints are provocative, engaging, and important. It is a privilege to present them.

At the Heart of Progress brings together the collector and the curator. The resulting exhibition and catalogue – conceived collaboratively and realized by the Ackland's curator of collections, Timothy Riggs – offer a thoughtful and well-researched introduction to the works, giving voice to the context in which these works were created, and directing our attention to the subtle and sublime messages embedded in the lines, shapes, colors, and subject matter.

At the Ackland, we believe that works of art create opportunities to understand the world around us. At this moment in our global history, *At the Heart of Progress* provides an exceptional starting point for conversations in classrooms and seminars across the campus of The University of North Carolina at Chapel Hill, in our public schools, and in our homes. The exhibition asks us to consider what lies at the heart of our progress and at what price.

On behalf of the Ackland, and all the audiences we serve, I express my deepest thanks to John, his wife Susan, and extended family for sharing these works with us.

Emily Kass
Director

Acknowledgments

from John P. Eckblad, Collector

First and foremost, I thank Susie Eckblad, Tim Riggs, Amanda Hughes, and the entire Ackland staff for their deep commitment to this project. Susie's constant support has enabled me to put together this collection, Tim's enthusiasm, curiosity, and perseverance have given us all a truly fresh look at industrialization and its implications, and Amanda's belief in the project and her management of the preparations have made this exhibition possible.

I thank the following people for opening doors for me in the preparation of this exhibition and the building of this collection: Tom Bier for inviting me into the work world of heavy industry; Vanina Eckblad for introducing me into the heart of the Paris art world; Joshua Eckblad for guiding me through the potentialities and vagaries of electronic databases; Martine, Ben and Ginny, Chris, Melissa, Megan and Sarah Rader for their strong and continuing support; Michele Badia for helping us understand the history and significance of Le Creusot; Paul McCarron, Stanley Crowe, Mireille Romand, and Arsene Bonafous-Murat for guiding my selection of prints and posters; and Verna Jerrell and Rhonda Rangeo for teaching me print and poster care, matting, and framing.

I also thank Jean-Baptiste Secheret, Craig McPherson, Pascale Hémery, Raymond Mason, and Maurice Culot for their time, interest, and insightful observations on art, industry, prints, and printmaking.

In addition, I express my gratitude to Ackland director, Emily Kass, who empowered her team to make the exhibition, programming, and this publication a reality.

from Timothy A. Riggs, Curator of Collections

I have wanted to mount an exhibition from John Eckblad's collection ever since he walked into my office and introduced himself eighteen years ago. The project has become a reality thanks to the support of Emily Kass and the assistance of many members of the Museum staff.

Comments from Carolyn Wood and Barbara Matilsky helped me refine my initial ideas for the exhibition and give it focus. In the registrars' department, Anita Heggli and Scott Hankins ably facilitated the loan of nearly a hundred books and prints (and one wind-up toy). Lyn Koehnline gave the objects conservation treatment when needed, and worked with Kristin Robinson and Kirby Sewell to ensure that they were appropriately matted and framed. I owe a special debt of gratitude to Kirby for unframing certain works at the last minute, to permit additional photography for the catalogue!

As usual Joe Gargasz has provided an exhibition design that will show off the work to best advantage. As this catalogue goes to press, I look forward with eager anticipation to the physical installation that he will contrive, together with Kirby Sewell and Andrew Nagy. Lauren Sanford gave valuable help in preparing the exhibition checklist and labels. Leslie Balkany and other members of the education department, working with Alison Hafera Cox, graduate intern, Jocelyn Arem, director of public programs, and with Susan Eckblad, have devised a broad range of interpretive programs to go with the exhibition.

Among her many contributions to this project, Amanda Hughes defined the scope and form of this catalogue, which has been designed by The Splinter Group. Peter Geoffrion photographed the objects for the catalogue, and Nic Brown gave valuable assistance with reproduction rights. My wife Carolyn read the essay in manuscript well before it was fit to turn over to an editor, and gave encouragement when I needed it most.

Above all, of course, I am grateful to John and Susan Eckblad for their hospitality over the years as I have visited the collection, for their generosity in entrusting a large part of it to the Museum for close study over the past year, and for their research in Europe which provided new and vital information about several of the prints in the exhibition.

Collector's Statement

When I was nine years old, my family moved from the birch-bordered lakes of Minnesota to the coal mining hills of western Pennsylvania. In my life, this qualified as a sea change. Fields and plains were replaced by traffic and heavy industry. My ideas and dreams of the world of work became more diversified and intriguing.

As a college student, I drove an ice cream truck in the summer to earn spending money. Around 10 P.M. each evening, I would park my truck in front of Duquesne's U.S. Steel Works. There the dancing orange flames of the open-hearth furnace always elevated my spirit. Turning 180 degrees from the ferocious light, I could see the tightly terraced rows of workers' homes. How did it feel to live this view? What were the effects of entering and exiting this sublime landscape daily in order to put food on the family table? How could one ever escape the blast furnace's presence? These memories have become a constant reference. Now, for over 35 years I've continued to search for similarly captivating views in life and art.

As a management consultant to large petrochemical complexes in northeastern England and northern Europe, my professional life was framed by cooling towers, pipe bridges, cat crackers, methane fermenters, machine works, and nuclear power plants. While I do not fully understood how these things work, I have never ceased to be entranced by their color, intensity, size, complexity, power, and movement. Being ignorant of the intricacies of the technology has not gotten in the way of feeling its majesty.

Somewhere in northern England in about 1974, I purchased my first print of what has become a significant collection of works on paper depicting various aspects of the Industrial Revolution. As I have gotten older, I have generally found it increasingly difficult to summon up the sensations that I once felt. These works on paper have made it possible for me to retrieve these fleeting, yet powerful, experiences.

This exhibition features prints and posters from my collection that depict the nature of life and work in and around the production and utilization of coal. These views start with the mining of coal, move on to the manufacture of iron and steel, and surface in the transformation of our country's vistas, transportation systems, and commercial products.

Today, with our economy and environment under siege, it's useful to remember that crisis begets invention. When we seem closest to capitulation, the seeds of our next reality have already been sown. And, we need not wonder for long how our new realities will look and feel. Once again, artists will be there to both document and interpret.

I hope that this exhibition communicates some of the wonder and excitement that I feel every time I think of the work places I've known or look at prints and posters that evoke these memories.

John P. Eckblad

At The Heart of Progress
Introduction

There are many histories of the Industrial Revolution; this is not one of them. Instead, this catalogue and the exhibition it accompanies are designed to explore a remarkable collection, assembled over the last three-and-a-half decades by John P. Eckblad on the subject of work and industry. Within the collection we have focused on heavy industry – the trinity of coal, iron, and steam. Between the 1750s and the 1950s that trinity, beginning as an exotic addition to human life, progressed to an all-encompassing framework for civilization. It did not begin the industrial revolution: that had already begun in British textile mills, with machines for spinning and weaving that were powered by waterwheels and mostly constructed of wood. But it drastically changed the scale and pace of industrial development, transforming the economy, the appearance, and the culture of Europe and America during the nineteenth and twentieth centuries.

The Eckblad collection records the ways that many different artists – and different kinds of artists – have looked at industry and labor over a period of more than two centuries. A collection focused on a single theme, particularly one as broad and potent as the history of industry, raises two questions. First, what can we learn from what we see in these pictures about the way the world looked at different times? The exhibition, and the checklist in this publication, are arranged to show various aspects of the culture of progress: coal mining, the manufacture and use of iron and steel, or the life of the worker, for example. Second, what did the artists choose to show us, and why, and how? This essay looks at the collection from that point of view.

The how is the easiest to see, for it is embedded in every image. On the most basic level, the print techniques themselves trace the history of an industrial revolution in the multiplication of pictures. The favorite eighteenth-century method, etching or engraving on a copper plate, was superseded by steel engraving, lithography, wood engraving, and photogravure, all methods that enabled pictures to be printed faster and in larger numbers than ever before. In 1800 it was extraordinary for an illustration to appear in a magazine or newspaper, by 1850 it was no longer uncommon, and by 1890 it was the norm.

The first artists to depict the workings of industry were documentarians who might well have used cameras if photography had been invented. Often there was a division of labor (itself an elementary industrial concept) between the artist who designed a picture and the engraver who transformed it into printable form. As industry matured, in the later nineteenth and the twentieth centuries, an increasing number of "fine-art" painters, sculptors, and printmakers came to see it as a valid subject for them. Ironically their "handcrafted" prints were often more old-fashioned in the technique than the work of the documentarians. However, it would be a mistake to draw a firm line between art and documentation. Creativity and accuracy are complementaries, not opposites. In the world of the print, commercial, documentary, and artistic considerations often exist side by side.

What the prints represent may seem obvious; we are not dealing with arcane or highly abstract images.

But identifying an industrial process, or the site of a factory view, is not always obvious. And once we have the answers to these questions we still may ask, is this a literal view or an idealization? Even an old advertisement may carry messages that were obvious to those who first looked at it but elude us.

Just why these prints were created is the most difficult question to answer. Who commissioned these images? What audience did the artist or publisher have in mind? But even when the artist is silent (and some have been very vocal) and the print lacks an explanatory caption, we may be able to guess at its intention from what we know about the history and the society of the time and place where it was issued.

The Volcano in the Countryside

To a twenty-first-century viewer the most striking thing about the early views of industry in the collection may be their rural mood. Today we tend to associate heavy industry with cities like Detroit and Pittsburg in America, or Birmingham and Sheffield in England. But until railroads were built, heavy freight like coal and iron ore could not travel any distance except by water: rivers or canals. Much of the earliest industry developed away from existing centers of population, near the necessary raw materials (coal and iron ore in particular) and the waterways that could transport them. Eventually a city might grow up around the industry.

As it happened, the early development of industry in England coincided with a growing interest in landscape among artists and art lovers. In particular, wild mountain scenery, previously seen as ugly or terrifying, came to be valued precisely for its ability to thrill the beholder, just as people today are attracted by the safely controlled terror of amusement park rides or horror movies. The concept of the overpowering "sublime" as an alternative to the pleasing "beautiful," came to be seen as a desirable quality in art. Mount Vesuvius erupted four times in the later eighteenth century and several artists recorded the combination of mountain and fire. England had no volcanoes, but the furnaces of an ironworks offered a scenic equivalent, with liquid iron for lava and an abundance of smoke and flame (see fig.2).

> Incessant night and day each crater roars
> Like the volcano on Sicilian shores
> Their fiery wombs each molten mass combine,
> Thence, lava like, the boiling torrents shine
> Down the trenched sand the liquid metal holds
> Shoots showers of stars and fills the hollow moulds.[1]

Coalbrookdale, a small town in the west of England, had been a center for iron smelting (the transformation of ore into iron) since the seventeenth century, and was the scene of major innovations in the production of iron, including the use of coke (processed coal) rather than charcoal. These innovations made iron cheaper and available in larger quantities, leading to its first large-scale use as a building material, the Coalbrookdale Iron Bridge of 1780 (Catalogue no. 4). Artists produced scenic views of the valley and its industry as early as the 1750s. Shortly after 1800 Philip James de Loutherbourg created one of the most dramatic (fig.1), issued in print form as part of a series titled *The Romantic and Picturesque Scenery of England and Wales*. Loutherbourg was both

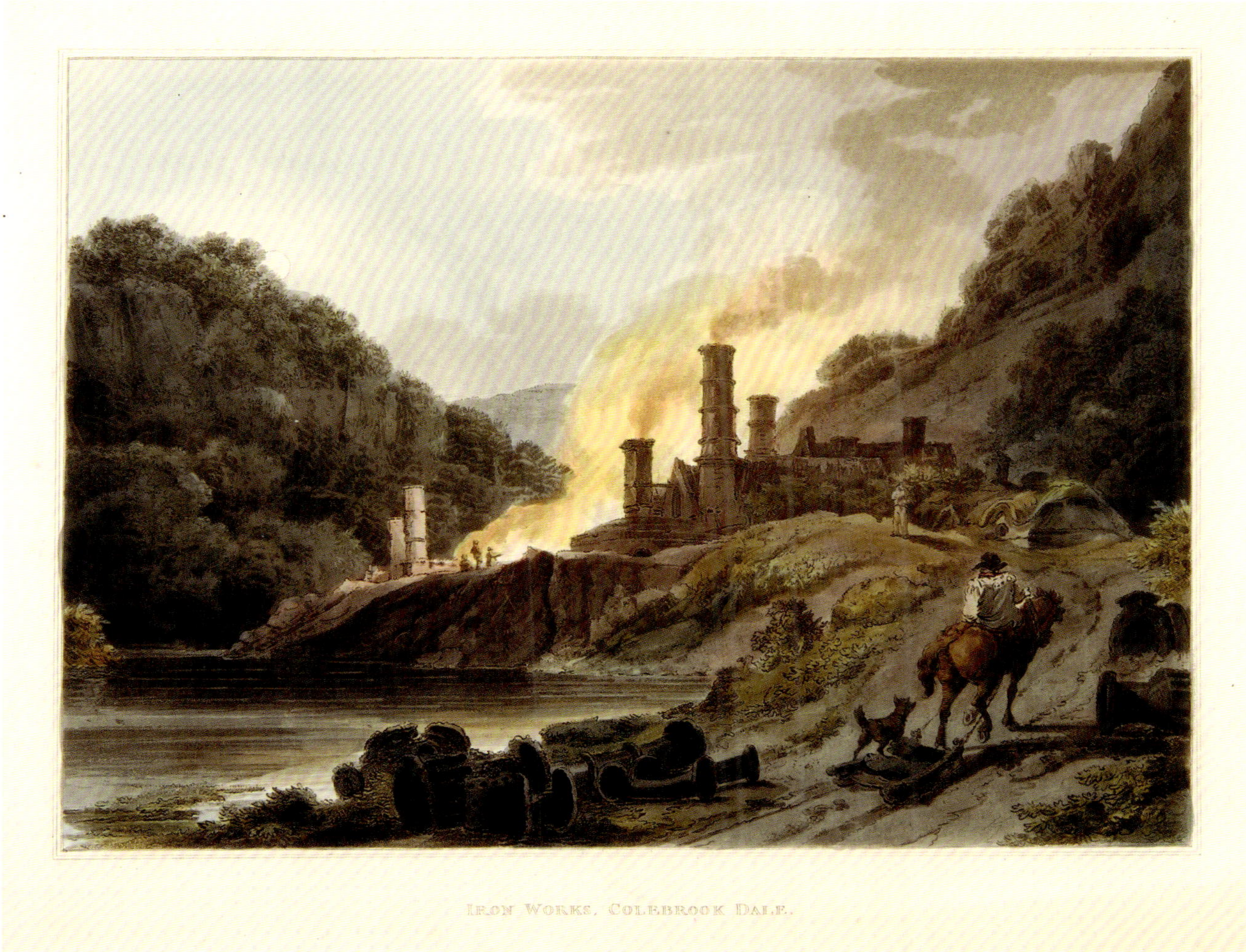

1. Philip James de Loutherbourg and William Pickett: *Iron Works, Colebrookdale*, 1805; aquatint, hand-colored. Catalogue no. 6

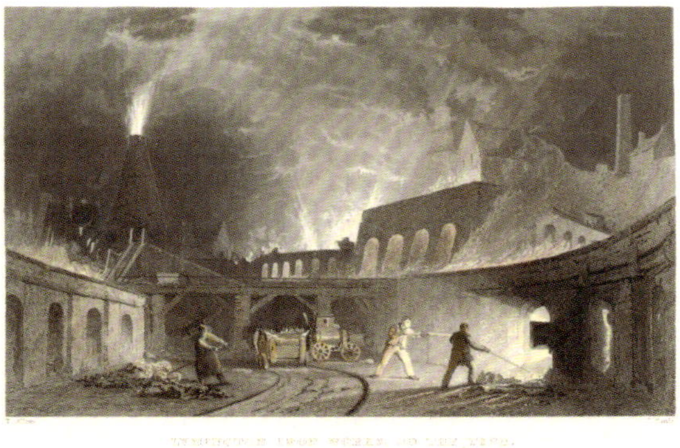

2. Thomas Allom and James Sands: *Lymington Iron Works on the Tyne*, 1832; engraving, hand-colored. Catalogue no. 35

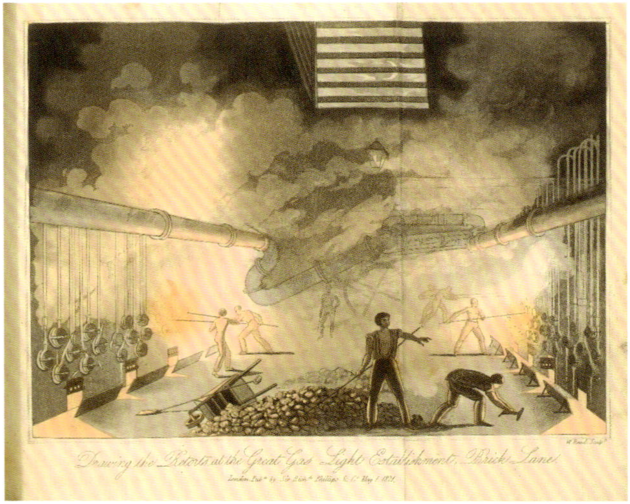

3. William Read: *Drawing the Retorts, Brick Lane Gas Works*, 1821; aquatint, hand-colored. Catalogue no. 47

a painter and a designer of theater sets, noted for spectacular effects of light, and he treated his subject accordingly. The actual process of iron working is invisible; we see only smoke, flame, and chimneys that suggest castle towers. The fragments of machinery in the foreground suggest the broken stones and carvings that often appear in eighteenth-century prints of ancient ruins. The straight lines and finished surfaces that we associate with modern machinery are nowhere to be seen.

A later view of the same type of industry is both more informative and more sinister: Thomas Allom's *Lymington Iron Works on the Tyne* (fig.2) from *Durham and Northumberland Illustrated*. The hand-coloring on this print may have been added later, but even in black and white Allom's image is hellish. Choosing a night view means that all the light in the picture is supplied by flame, and unlike Loutherbourg, Allom has moved closer to his subject, until everything visible is part of the industrial environment. We can even determine the process depicted here. Because iron smelted with coke contained impurities that made it brittle, it was worked – "wrought" – by hand-stirring the liquid metal in the furnace, burning or skimming off the undesirable material. The men in the foreground with long poles are engaged in this work, known as puddling. One historian has described puddling as "the heaviest regular task ever accepted by man"[2] and another calls puddlers "the aristocracy of the proletariat, proud, clannish, set apart by sweat and blood. Few of them lived past forty."[3] The wrought iron that puddling produced was the material of choice for ships, locomotives, machines, and heavy construction until ways of manufacturing steel in quantity were developed after 1860.

Coal, iron, and steam power came together in a complicated triangular relationship. As ironworks increased the demand for coal, coal mines were dug ever deeper, and the danger of flooding made pumping apparatus a necessity. Thomas Newcomen created the earliest steam-powered pump for coal mines in 1712. Although it was inefficient and used enormous amounts of coal, the Newcomen engine was practical because it could be fed with unsalable waste from the mine it was pumping out. The early Newcomen engines used surprisingly little iron in their construction, but as iron became cheaper and available in larger quantities, the cylinders of the later Newcomen engines were made of iron instead of brass, and the vastly improved engine devised by James Watt in the 1770s depended on iron cylinders fabricated with unprecedented precision. Watt's engine was an efficient source of power beyond the coal fields, for machinery as well as for pumping.

Iron demanded coal, coal demanded steam, steam demanded more and better iron, but this circle of progress was soon sending out branches. Coke, the key to iron-smelting with coal, was produced by baking coal in ovens to increase its carbon content by vaporizing other components. The by-product, coal-gas, was soon found to have its own uses as a fuel and a source of light. An early technical illustration (fig.3) shows the process of gas production: the coked coal is being raked out of the retorts where its gas content has been boiled off. Like Allom, William Read has selected a night scene, perhaps to emphasize the use of gas for street-lighting (notice the moon glimpsed though a skylight). The general mood is almost as infernal as in Allom's design, but in the smaller space of the gas-works human figures seem more the masters and less the slaves of their surroundings. A workman in the center, with legs spread and commanding gesture, dominates the scene.

Transportation was an even more important offshoot of the coal-iron-steam triangle. Even over the best gravel roads, it was a hopeless effort to transport heavy freight like coal for any great distance. Therefore, for centuries special roads had been made in mining areas to carry coal out of the mine, or from the mine to a waterway – roads using wooden rails and wagons built to run on them. By 1767 the Coalbrookdale ironworks was making cast-iron rails for these "rail-ways," and 1804 saw the first use of a steam engine to replace the horses that had pulled the wagons. Beginning in 1820 wrought-iron rails

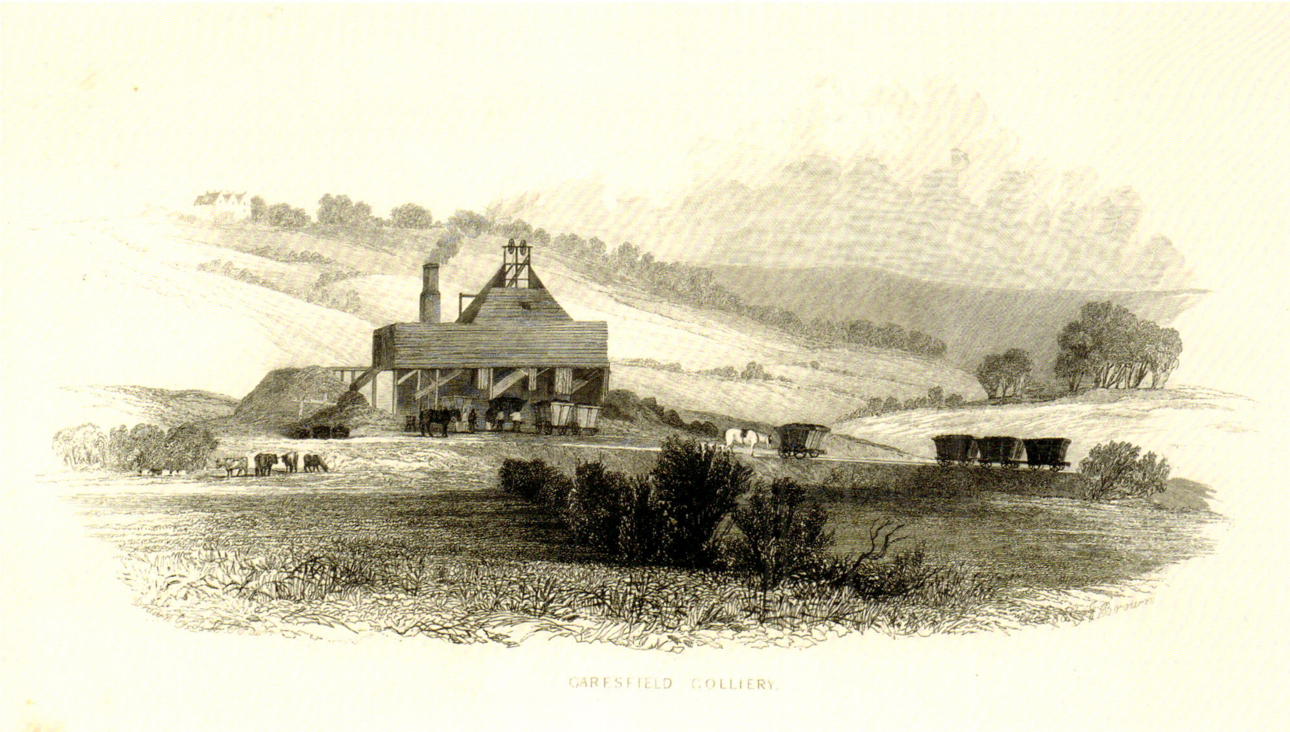

4. Thomas H. Hair: *Garesfield Colliery*, 1839; etching. Catalogue no. 7

5. John Cooke Bourne: *Berkhampstead, Herts. June 10th 1837*, 1839; lithograph in black and gray. Catalogue no. 53

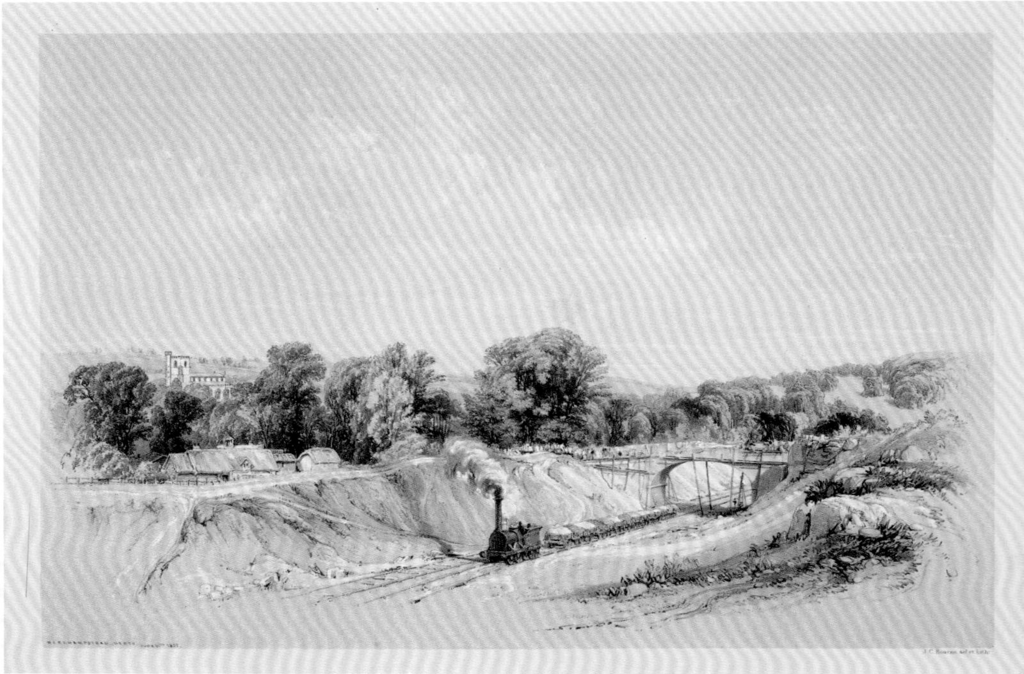

6. George Hawkins the younger: *Britannia Bridge*, 1848; color lithograph. Catalogue no. 43

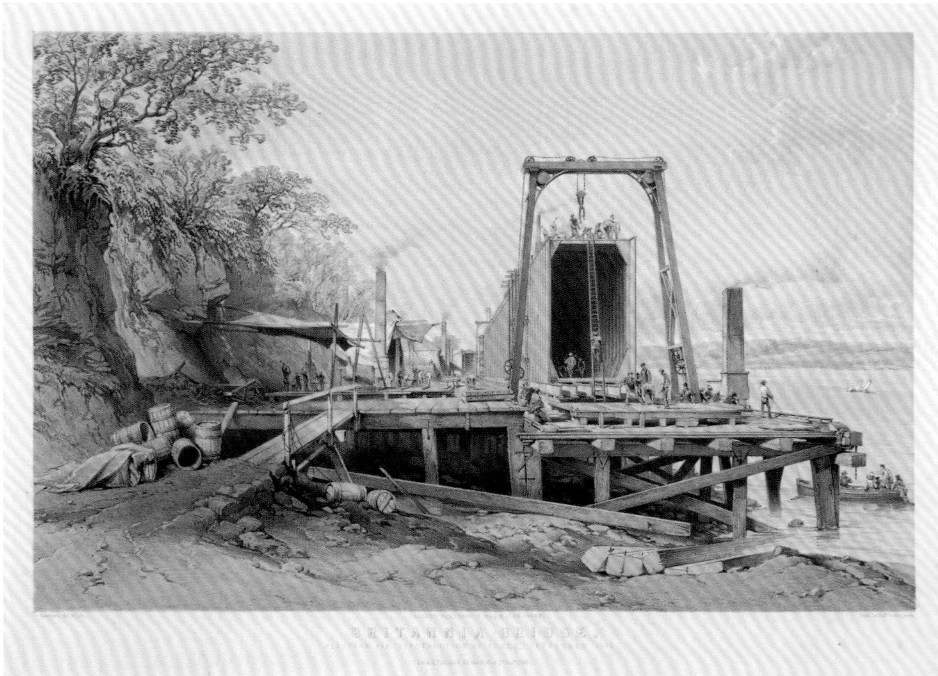

replaced the less durable cast iron, and by 1821 visionaries were imagining a system that could be built to carry freight and passengers all over England.

The view of a coal mine by Thomas Hair (fig.4), from 1839, gives a typical example of the early horse-drawn railroad. Apart from the rails and coal wagons, *Garesfield Colliery* might be a farm nestled in a peaceful valley. Only a closer look reveals the hoist machinery emerging from the roof, the chutes for coal, and the fact that the horses are there to haul coal rather than to plow. The print comes from a series, *The Mines of Durham and Northumberland*, that Hair presented with some hesitancy, acknowledging that "whilst the eloquent pens of the tourist, the merchant, the politician, and the statist have found themes of wonder, of interest, and of deep consideration in descanting upon them [the mines], their appearance has been considered to possess so little of attraction, or rather to be so repulsive, as to forbid the investigations of the artist."[4] Nevertheless, Hair clearly hoped to convince the viewer that his views deserved artistic consideration. The series as a whole offers a wide range of topography and mood: desolate moorland and night views with flaring fires alternate with river and harbor scenes where coal "drops" load boats or ships, and collieries like Garesfield surrounded by cattle, sheep, or cultivated land. The irregular timber-framed buildings of the collieries vary widely, but several, like Garesfield, suggest the picturesque farm buildings of traditional rural landscape.

The first inter-city railroad opened in 1830, between the manufacturing towns of Liverpool and Manchester; significantly, a railroad linking London to another city would not open for another eight years. But by the time that John Cooke Bourne published his views of that railroad in 1839, *Drawings of the London and Birmingham Railway*, there were as many as ten other railroads out of London under construction. As railroads continued to spread across England in the 1830s and 1840s, a new quality was introduced into the landscape, the sublimity of the straight line. High land values, cheap labor, and engineering constraints led British engineers to lay out their routes in as straight a line as possible, regardless of topography. Hills were cut or tunneled, valleys filled or bridged. Traditionally long unbroken straight lines had not been considered desirable in a landscape composition; even a shore or seascape seldom presented the unbroken horizon line, interrupting it instead with objects in the foreground. A towering mountain or breaking wave might be sublime, but a flat plain or calm sea was simply monotonous. But the man-made straight line, carried to unprecedented length carried with it a suggestion of human power and grandeur that rivaled the natural sublime. Bourne's lithographs, documenting the construction of the railroad, contrast the gentle curves of the natural landscape with the clean straight line of the rails cutting through it (fig.5). In other prints from the series the long horizontal of an embankment or viaduct, or the receding perspective of a series of identical activities as workmen dig a cut through a hill, introduce the new aesthetic.

A still more striking example is George Hawkins' view of the construction of the Britannia railroad bridge ten years later (fig.6). This time the peaceful landscape is invaded by one of the gigantic wrought-iron tube trusses, each more than four hundred fifty feet long, that would span the Menai Strait in Wales. The dramatic contrast between the irregular wooden scaffolding around the tube and the precision and abrupt perspective of the tube itself must have struck viewers in the 1840s as it strikes us, but for us it is the scaffolding that looks quaint – for them the tube must have had the exotic quality of a visitor from another world.

France, Germany, and the rest of Continental Europe were slow to follow the British lead in industrialization. Geographical and political barriers hindered commerce, natural resources were more scattered, and transportation was more primitive. Only after 1850, as railroad networks solved the problem of transportation, did the major continental nations begin to catch up with England. Before that industrial development occurred in isolated pockets, and the rural quality of industry persisted longer than in Britain.

The region of Le Creusot in France is a good example of early local development. Coalfields, deposits of iron ore, and a major waterway (the Canal du Centre, opened in 1793) facilitated the development of an iron industry. Created in the 1780s under the sponsorship of the French government, the foundry of Le Creusot appears in an engraving (fig.7) that probably shows

7. Anonymous, French: *View of the foundry and Forges at Le Creusot*, 1780s (printed after 1790); etching. Catalogue no. 33

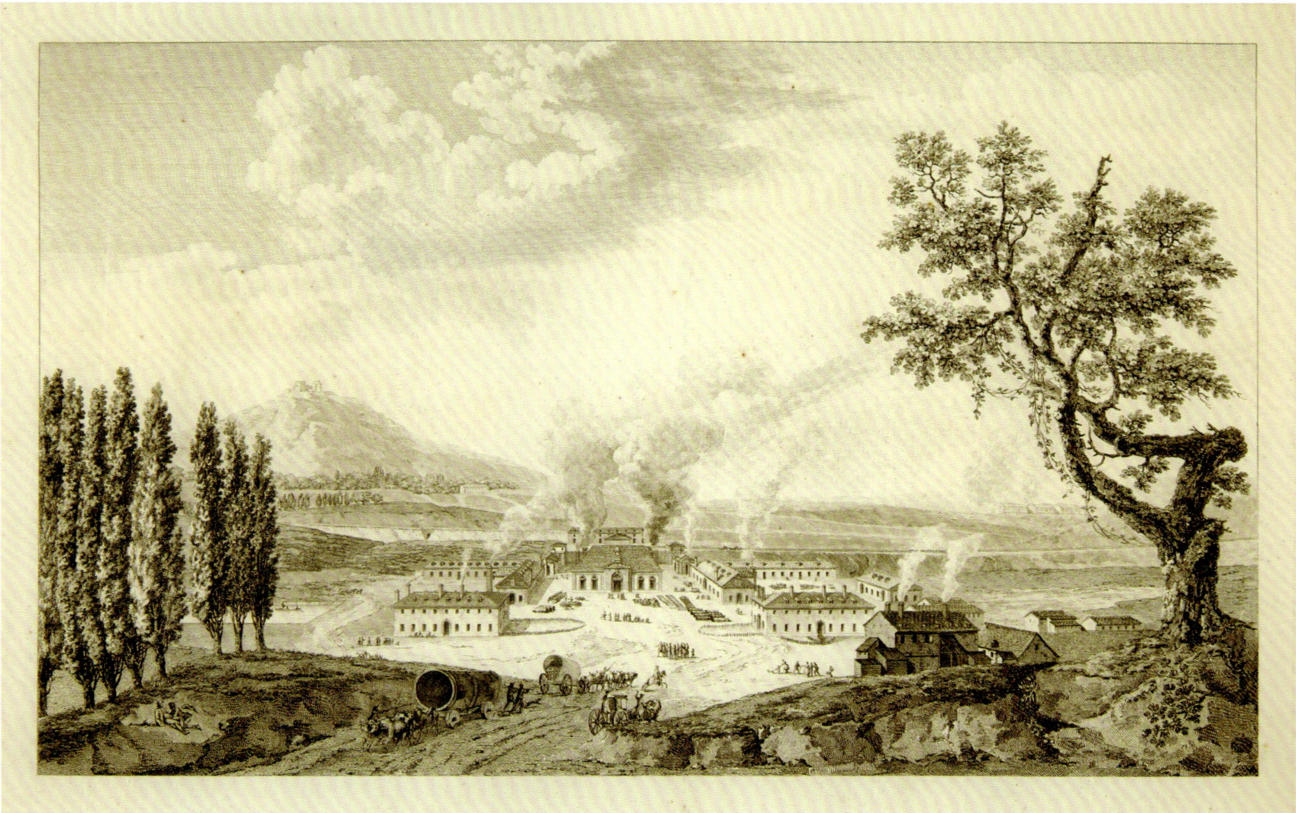

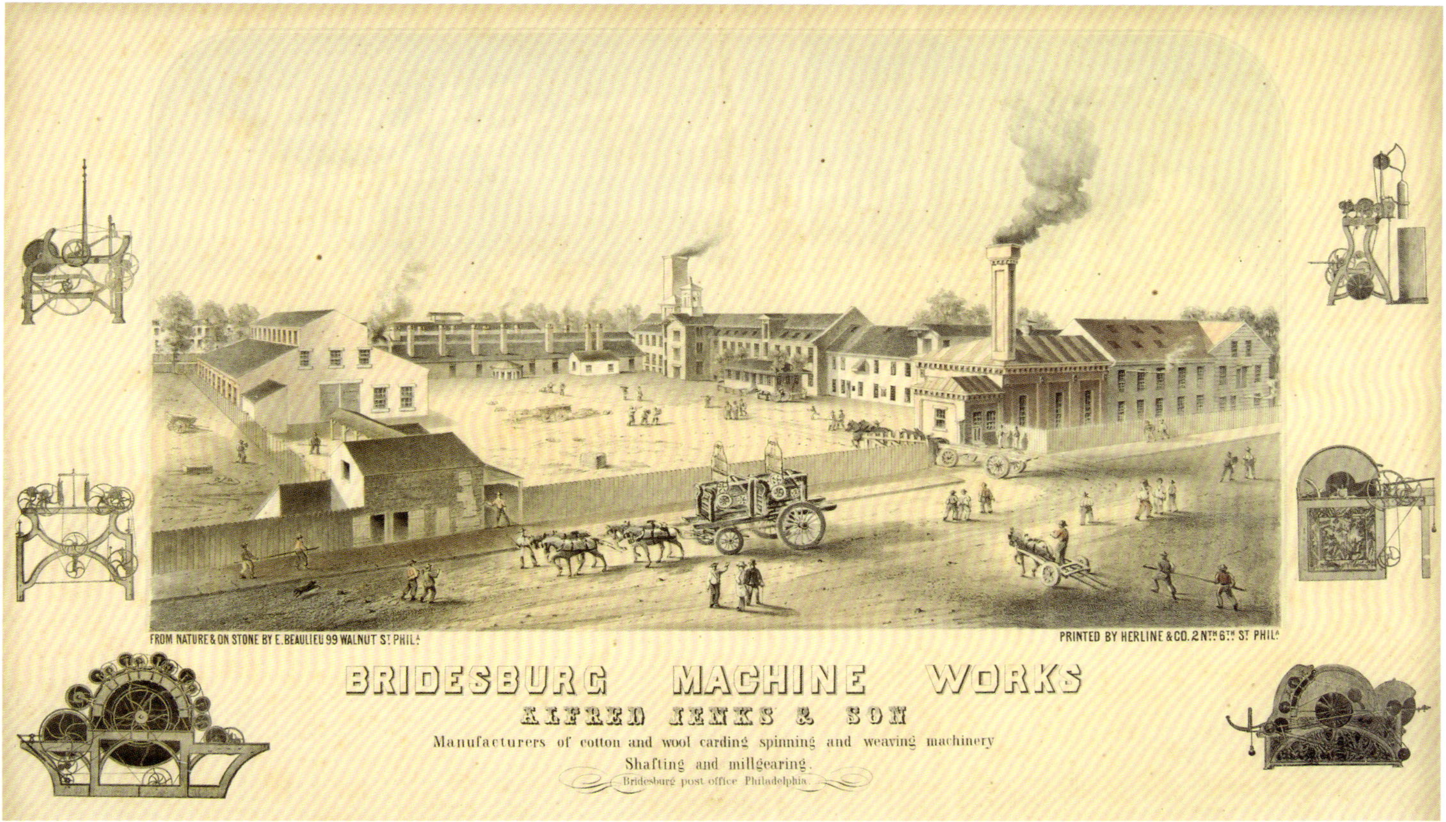

8. Emile Beaulieu: *Bridesburg Machine Works*, 1856; color lithograph. Catalogue no. 45

the buildings in their original state.[5] The complex has the grandeur and symmetry of a chateau. Anchors and cannon lying in the courtyard emphasize the foundry's role in sustaining French military power. The artist has surrounded the buildings with an elegant setting quite different from Loutherbourg's romantic vision of British industry, and evidently the product of the artist's imagination; the trees have the look of stage scenery and the conspicuous mountain in the distance is missing from later views of the same site. The most novel element in the view is easy to pass over: the huge tube moving on a cart in the foreground is probably the cylinder of a Newcomen steam pump, destined for one of the nearby coal mines. The early steam pumps required enormous cylinders, six feet in diameter and more than ten feet long, and a similar one appears in the foreground of a 1758 view of Coalbrookdale (Catalogue no. 1). Le Creusot was in fact an industrial pioneer, the first French ironworks to use coke instead of charcoal and to make serious use of steam power, but it was slow to develop. Major expansion began only after 1836 under the leadership of the Schneider family.

There are interesting parallels and differences between the view of Le Creusot and Emile Beaulieu's

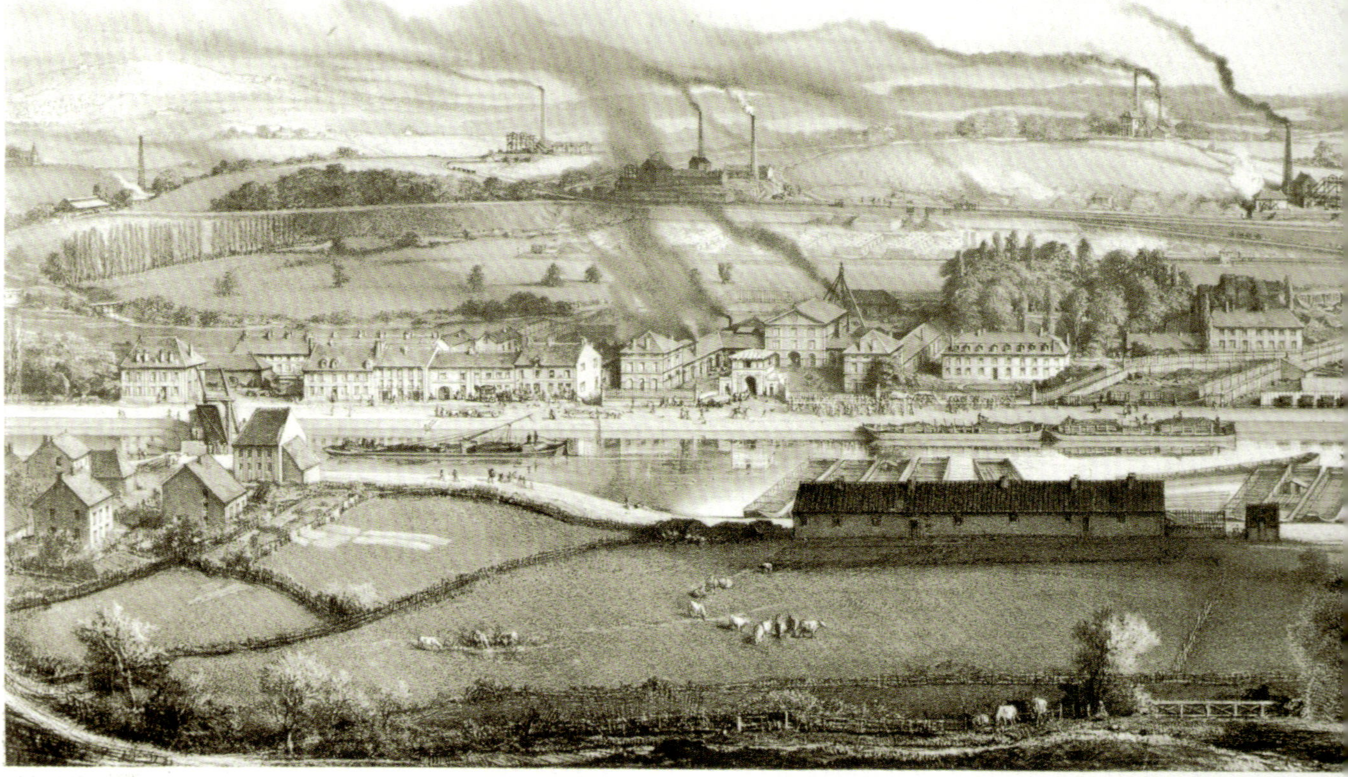

9. Ignace François Bonhommé: *Montceau-les-Mines*, 1857; lithograph in black and brown. Catalogue no. 9

view of an American factory (fig.8) half a century later. Little is known of the artist, though his name suggests that he was an immigrant from France. His oblique view of the factory complex suits its more informal layout, and in place of the elegant ornamental landscape framing Le Creusot, we have an actual frame displaying the machines produced by the factory. This is of course an advertising poster, but in its way, so is the view of Le Creusot. The difference in tone is not so much a difference in purpose as a difference in audience: on the one hand the French patriot interested in the grandeur of his nation and its enterprises, and on the other the matter-of-fact American businessman who might buy the machines produced by the Bridesburg Machine Works.

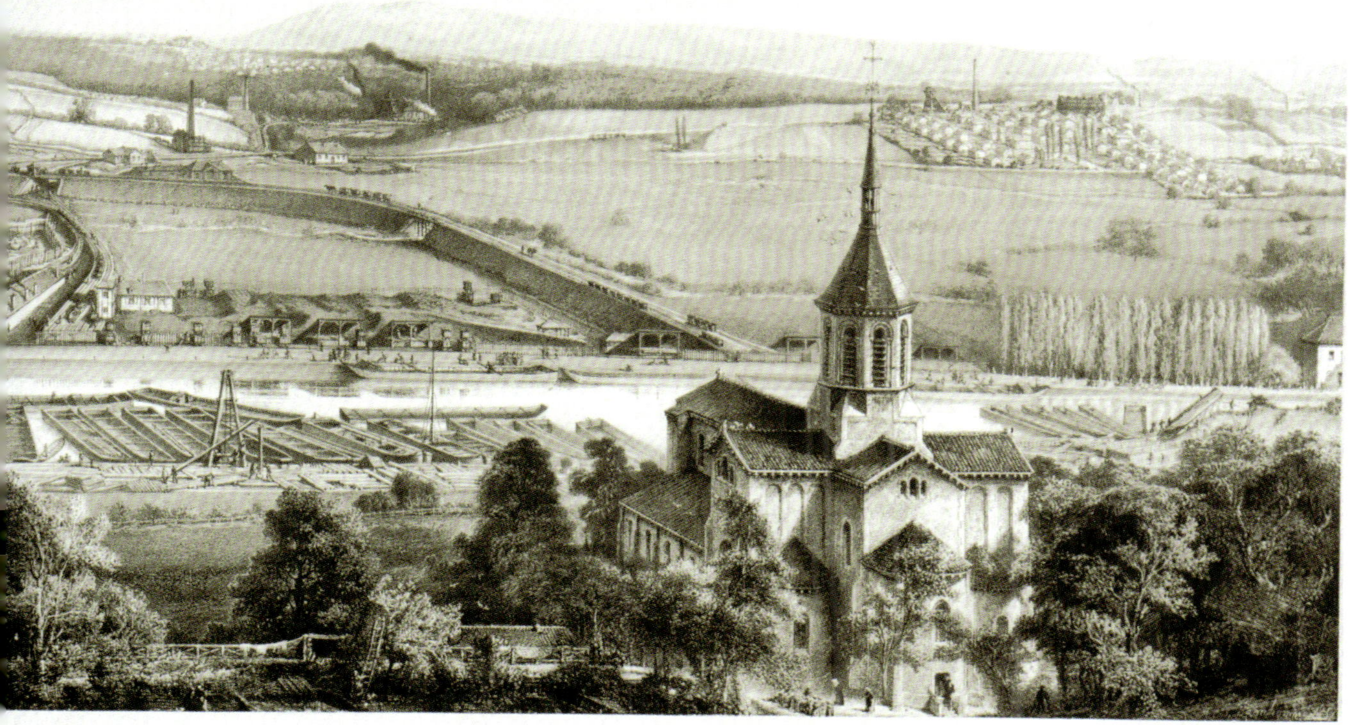

A similar contrast appears when we compare the American print to a mid-nineteenth-century French print of the Le Creusot region. François Bonhommé's print *Montceau* (fig.9) belongs to a group made in 1857, depicting the coal fields of Blanzy that fed the furnaces of Le Creusot. Early in his career Bonhommé had made lithographs for the *Voyages pittoresques et romantiques dans l'ancienne France*, a vast publication that set out to document the architecture and scenery of France province by province. The compilers of the *Voyages pittoresques* had no interest in modern constructions, but in the 1850s Bonhommé committed himself to depicting industrial sites. His print gives the convincing panorama of a tract of country, dotted with the pitheads of coal mines and centering on the little town of Montceau-les-Mines on the Canal du Centre.

It is highly likely that Bonhommé's project was subsidized by the Chagot family, who had controlled the coal fields since 1818. François Léonce Chagot (1822-1893) who became mayor of Montceau-les-Mines in 1856, saw it as his duty both to promote the welfare of his employees and to control their behavior. Bonhommé's print is not a simple advertisement like the American view, but a more elevated piece of propaganda, suggesting an orderly society. The streaming smoke, which present-day viewers are likely to see in terms of environmental damage, would have been a sign of prosperity; the mines are active and the miners employed. The canal with its coal barges and the well-constructed town carry the same message. The distant settlement to the right is a company town, the "workers' town of Alouettes" (*cité ouvrière des Alouettes*); in another print from the series (Catalogue no. 8), a similar village is identified as "the village of Le Magny, constructed by the Company for its workers, with school and chapel." The print of Montceau also includes anticipated improvements, including a gatehouse in front of the company's central offices (never built) and the imposing church in the right foreground, on which construction was just beginning.

The future church is an important part of the print's message. The struggle between the Catholic Church and its secular opponents was a major issue in French cultural and political life throughout the nineteenth century, and in this struggle the Chagot family were "clericals" who saw Catholicism both as the true religion and as a desirable agent of social control. Bonhommé's own political sympathies were probably divided between the workers and the industrialists who controlled them; he often signed himself Bonhommé-Forgeron (Bonhommé-Blacksmith) and created many sympathetic images of workers. *Montceau*, however, offers an almost utopian view of paternalistic capitalism, where the masters give the workers what is good for them. The next half-century would see a frequent contrast between images like this and others that depicted the tension between capital and labor within the industrial landscape.

Triumph and Suffering

Historians of the Industrial Revolution see it entering a new phase between 1850 and 1875. Outside England railroads were still an exceptional form of transportation in 1850; in the next two decades they crossed Europe and America with a network of transport lines. The revolution in transportation helped continental nations (France, Belgium, and Germany in particular) to overcome barriers to industrialization. With the United States, they came to rival Britain as industrial powers by the end of the century. Also thanks to the railroad, industrial sectors began to develop around traditional urban centers like Paris.

Progress became systematic. In Europe, scientific and technological institutions, often established with government support, began to supersede the inspired tinkering of the earliest generation of inventors and engineers. In the United States, Thomas Edison effectively created a factory for producing inventions. Machines made of iron, with standardized parts, replaced the individually designed and constructed machinery of the early nineteenth century: the product line displayed by the Bridesburg Machine Works (fig.8) was a portent of the future. Increasingly, mass-produced steel replaced wrought iron as the primary material for machines and construction. Electricity emerged as an alternative to steam for power (although the electricity itself required coal-fired, steam-powered generators). The first practical internal-combustion engines (running on coal-gas) appeared in factories, and petroleum products, for lighting and eventually for fuel, gradually became available.

The scale of industry and the techniques employed changed. Mines, factories, and engines were dramatically larger. In 1829 an ocean-going steamer had 60 horsepower to turn its paddle wheels; in 1893 the twin propellers of an ocean liner could command 30,000 horsepower. A comparable change in the railroad can be measured in the contrast between Bourne's little train (fig.5) making its way through the English countryside and Luigi Kasimir's etching (Catalogue no. 54) of a huge German locomotive, speeding across an African landscape some time after 1900.

The industrialization of Europe coincided with an increasing interest in the artistic and literary exploration of industrial environment. Early literary views of industry, in the novels of Charles Dickens for example, envision it as an alien intrusion, for good or evil, on a stable traditional society. Dickens' central characters may be exposed to an industrial world, but they see it from the outside. In the 1850s *Punch*, the British humor magazine that was a barometer of middle-class values, depicted miners as picturesque roughnecks in a world set apart from polite society. A famous cartoon by John Leech shows two burly miners looking at a well-dressed man, with the caption: *First Polite Native*. "Who's 'im, Bill?" *Second ditto*. "A stranger!" *First ditto*. " 'Eave 'arf a brick at 'im."[6] Clearly the reader was expected to identify himself with the "stranger," and the expression " 'eave 'arf a brick" became proverbial. Thirty years later, in Emile Zola's novels *Germinal* (1885) and *La Bête humaine* (1890) the main characters are miners or railroad workers, and we see their world from the inside: not only through their actions but through their thoughts, hopes, and anxieties.

As industry changed from intruder to environment, the issue became how society was to respond to it. The giant mines and factories accentuated the gap between the millionaires at the top and the mass of workers at the bottom. One response to the triumph of industry was to condemn not the technology but the society that it had produced. As early as the 1820s the social philosopher Henri Saint Simon had proclaimed: "until now, man has exploited man ... man no longer exploits man, but man in association with man exploits the world, delivered into his power."[7] By the 1870s it was clear that this optimism was premature. Socialists, communists, and anarchists proposed various alternatives to the triumph of industrial capitalism.

Think of Impressionist painting, and the first vision in your mind is probably a tourist's landscape of beaches, sailboats, unspoiled countryside, or broad city boulevards. But both Manet and Monet included the technological landscape of steamboats and railroad sheds in their work. At least one Impressionist, Camille Pissarro, deliberately chose to depict the industrial landscape: several paintings and one print (fig.10) show a factory in the town of Pontoise where he was living in the 1870s. In contrast to Bonhommé's monumental lithograph of Montceau, a sophisticated cousin to the poster, Pissarro's little

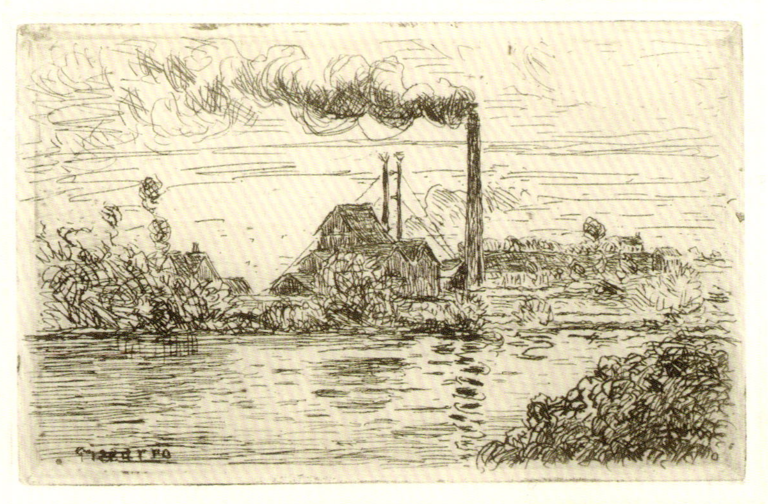

10. Camille Pissarro: *Factory at Pontoise*, 1874; etching. Catalogue no. 58

11. Maximilien Luce: *Rotterdam Harbor*, circa 1908; etching. Catalogue no. 64. © 2009 Artists Rights Society (ARS), New York/ADAGP, Paris

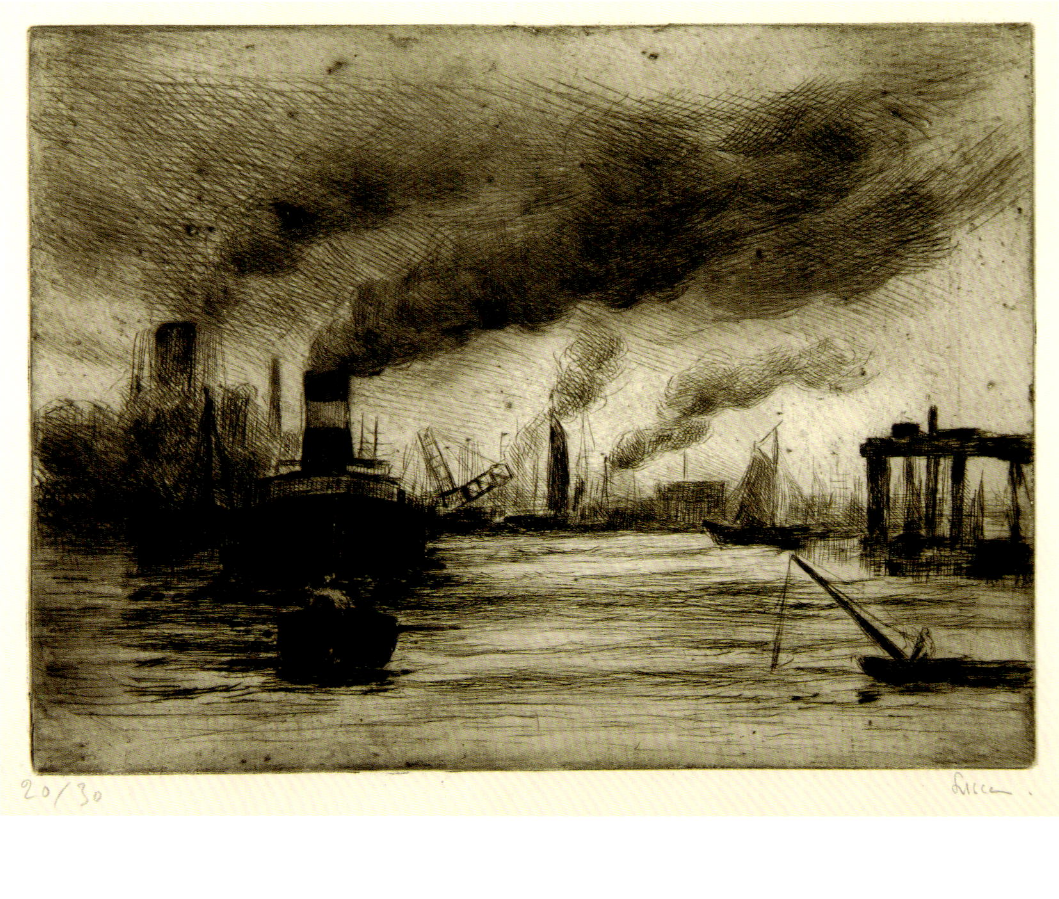

etching would have appealed to an audience of print collectors who might accept his view of a factory as an updated version of Rembrandt's windmills. And in contrast to Bonhommé's sculptural sense of the landscape, Pissarro dissolves it into patches of light and shadow: the reflections on the water are as substantial as the smokestack that casts them.

The choice of the small factory is probably not accidental. By the 1890s Pissarro was committed to the social philosophy of anarchism. Anarchism is usually remembered today for the terrorist bombings perpetrated by its most radical fringe, but the most serious anarchist thinkers believed in a peaceful revolution that would eventually produce a society of small communities, mingling industry, commerce, and agriculture. In 1874, when he made this print, Pissarro may not have been as familiar with anarchist thought as he was later, but he was probably acquainted with some of the social theories that led up to anarchism. From that point of view the small factory at Pontoise, rather than the giant industrial communities that were spreading across Europe, could be the sign of a better future.

Anarchism was also the chosen political stance of a younger generation of French artists, the Neo-Impressionists, who were much more interested in the urban industrial environment. Rotterdam Harbor by Maximilien Luce (fig.11) is a landscape dominated by smoke, the double-edged symbol of industrial development. On the one hand it was the sign of power and prosperity; on the other of pollution and death; its noxious effects had been recognized since the beginning of the nineteenth century. Isolated plumes against a clear sky convey an optimistic interpretation, while the gloomy pall of *Rotterdam Harbor* suggests a more skeptical view, blackening the sky and blowing towards the one remaining light area in the composition. Compared with the nervous, accomplished squiggles of Pissarro's etching, Luce's line-work is almost ostentatiously crude, as though the brutal power on display needed to be conveyed in a brutal manner.

Elisée Reclus, anarchist by conviction and geographer by profession, wrote that life in the city stimulates the mind but weakens the body.[8] The Belgian poet Emile Verhaeren, likewise sympathetic to anarchism, offered a similar view. Belgium was the first industrialized nation on the continent, and Verhaeren's poems of the 1890s described a world in which the countryside is a region of stagnation and ignorance, while the city, with its slums and pollution, is also a center of productive industry, intellectual life, and scientific research. Luce's image is similar to the one evoked in Verhaeren's poem "The Harbor":

> All of the sea's life goes toward the city!
>
> Its harbor is raining soot through the fog
> Where the sun like an eye, red and colossal, runs tears.
>
> Its harbor is a tumult of steamers that smoke
> And bellow, at the bottom of the night, unseen.[9]

A theater program illustration (fig.12) by another artist affiliated with the anarchist cause, H. G. Ibels, presents a more clearly negative landscape. Workmen shovel beneath a mountainous range of coal piles in an indeterminate setting. A green patch of waste ground and a wall topped by a street lamp suggest a factory environment on the outskirts of a city.

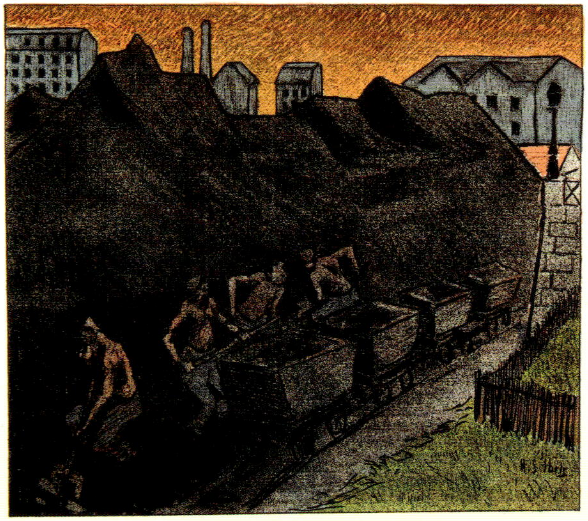

12. Henri-Gabriel Ibels: *Theater Program: "The Weavers"*, 1892/3; color lithograph. Catalogue no. 25

Ibels uses red and yellow effectively for an angry sky and the workers' bodies glow through the black of the modeling like flesh under coal dust. Why did Ibels make this image for Gerhart Hauptmann's play *The Weavers* (1892), a play about German craftsmen in the 1840s? The answer may be that by the 1890s the production and use of coal had become the archetypical image of oppressed labor. Rather than present a historical image of Hauptmann's weavers, Ibels has chosen to give playgoers a contemporary equivalent to their suffering and struggle.

In Jean Émile Laboureur's *The Factories* (fig.13) the landscape of urban industry is more naturalistically portrayed than in Ibels' synoptic view. An onlooker, whose patched trousers and idle pose mark him as an outsider to this landscape of industry, sits on high ground and stares at the distant forest of chimneys. Between is an empty space divided into sections, probably vegetable gardens for the city markets, and a straight road linking the factory zone to the city. The view apparently represents an industrial zone near the city of Nantes, but it resembles paintings by Luce and others of the Plaine de Saint Denis outside Paris, which by 1902 was on its way to becoming the leading industrial zone in France. The French name for this territory at the edge of the city, *banlieue*, is usually translated as suburb, but conveys a completely different environmental image. The print evokes another poem by Verhaeren, also called "Factories":

> Rectangles of granite and monuments of brick
> And long black walls going for miles
> With giant strides, through the *banlieues*;
> And on their roofs, in the fog, prickly
> with spikes and lightning rods,
> The smokestacks.[10]

A few years before Laboureur's vision of the *banlieue*, the symbolist printmaker Maurice Dumont had produced a more mysterious series of views of similar terrain, collectively titled *Surroundings of the City* (Autour de la ville). Willowy female figures, usu-

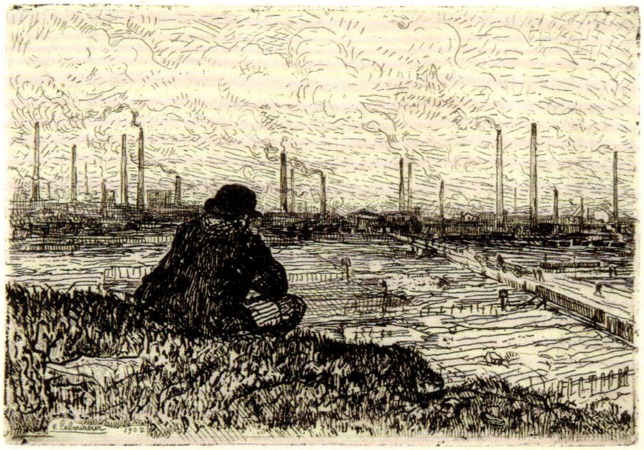

13. Jean Émile Laboureur: *The Factories*, 1902; etching. Catalogue no. 63. © 2009 Artists Rights Society (ARS), New York/ADAGP, Paris

ally haloed, stand in undefined spaces with distant landscape backgrounds. The small prints and stylized figures evoke medieval manuscript illuminations or fifteenth-century engravings, but the landscapes are the mostly desolate outskirts of a French city of the 1890s. Two figures in one of these prints (fig.14) hold a leafy branch: are they blessing the barren ground?

Dumont's juxtaposition of religious and industrial imagery must be seen in the light of the continuing struggle between clerical and anticlerical forces in France, which intensified in the later nineteenth century. Montceau-les-Mines, dominated by the church in Bonhommé's lithograph (fig.9), was the scene of an anticlerical riot in 1883, when workers destroyed religious imagery and attempted to dynamite a giant statue of the Virgin Mary. By the time of Dumont's etching, the Catholic Church, which initially had shown little sympathy for the condition of industrial workers, was making an effort to reach out to them. In 1891 Pope Leo XIII had issued an encyclical, *De Rerum Novarum* (Recent Happenings), calling on Catholics to consider the needs of the worker in response to the growing influence of movements like anarchism and socialism. Dumont's own religious convictions are unknown and probably were not orthodox, but his saintly figures suggest an effort to link spiritual life to the world of the factory.

A very different mood infuses the work of the American Joseph Pennell, who produced hundreds of prints and drawings of industrial scenes. Pennell's mantra was "the Wonder of Work" (his capitalization), which he felt had become the dominant subject for art in his own day, the equivalent of religion in an earlier age. He travelled across America and Europe from the 1880s to the 1920s, depicting industrial landscapes and engineering achievements like the building of the Panama Canal. Pennell and Luce share a sense of the brutal power of coal and steam, landscapes of energy and pollution that are heroic in their very inhumanity. But Pennell's political stance was far removed from anarchism; for him the awesome power of industry was its own justification. Pennell's etching *The Great Stack, Sheffield* (fig.15) is filled with smoke, but the giant stack at the center seems to imply the possibility of carrying it all far away. Significantly the great stack itself

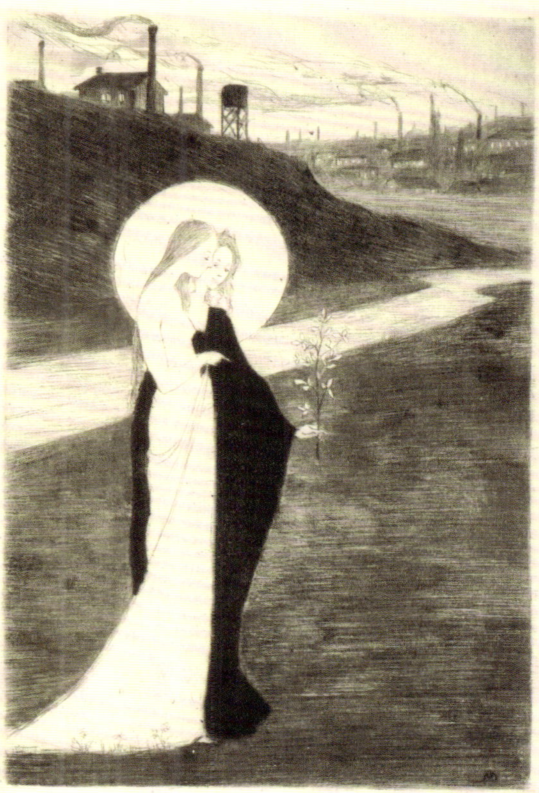

14. Maurice Dumont: *Untitled*, plate 4 from *Surroundings of the City*, 1895; drypoint and aquatint. Catalogue no. 67

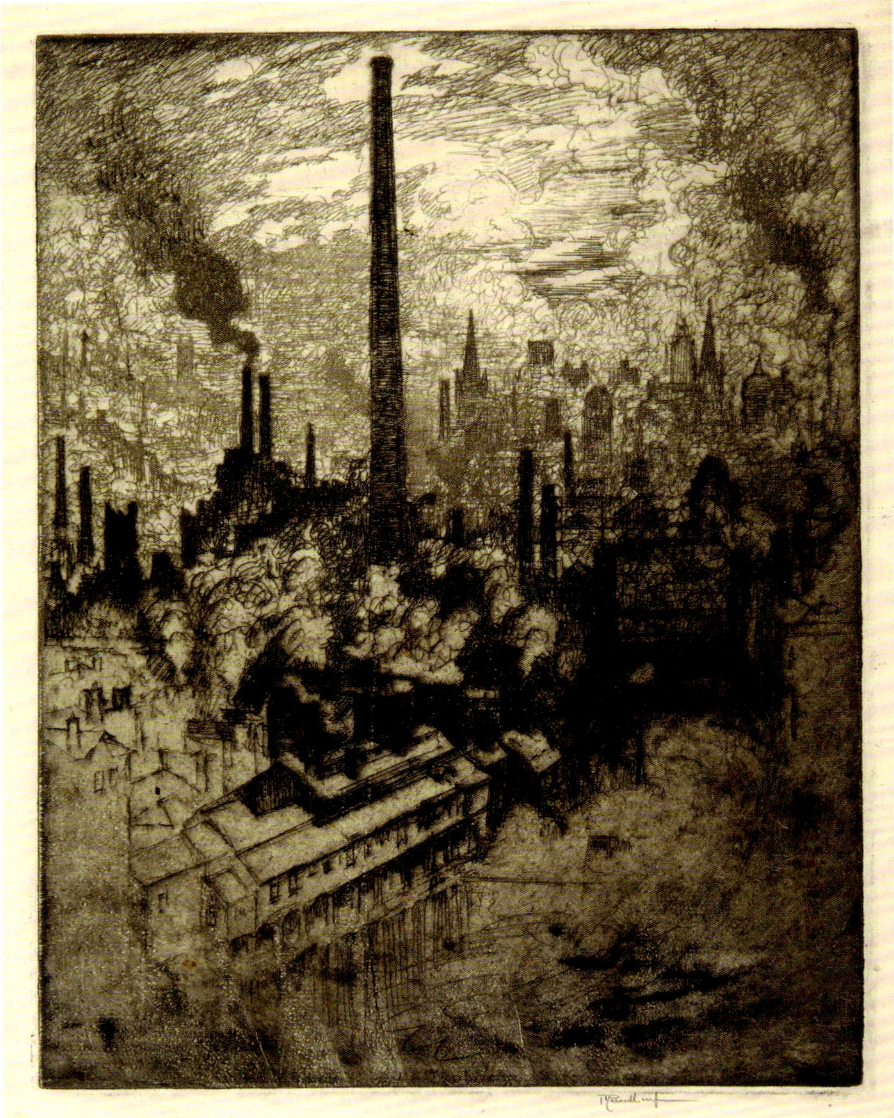

15. Joseph Pennell: *The Great Stack, Sheffield*, 1909; etching. Catalogue no. 59

The literary equivalent of Pennell's work is not the novels of Zola, but a story of 1895 by Rudyard Kipling, "The Ship that Found Herself." The story, a dialogue among the mechanical parts of a steamer on her maiden voyage, is an optimistic parable about the way humans combine to form a community. Pennell would surely have responded to Kipling's vision of society as a working machine where each part, from the capstan on deck to the smallest rivet holding the keel, knows its proper place – and if not, that is its own fault. To judge from his comments on his own prints, Pennell had little interest in the working conditions that accompanied industrial development. Writing about Sheffield he remarks: "Two things always impressed me in that town – the boiling water in the rivers and the abominable habits of the natives in the streets, who from across the rivers and behind walls and other safe places ''eave 'arf a brick' at you if you dare to draw."[11]

emits no smoke, and it emerges into a light sky from the murk below, which the artist has accentuated by leaving a heavy film of ink on the surface of his printing plate.

Frederick Detwiller's lithograph *The Spur* (fig.16) depicts demolition work on a New York elevated train line with an enthusiasm similar to Pennell's. By 1924 the "El" was a familiar sight, and clearing part

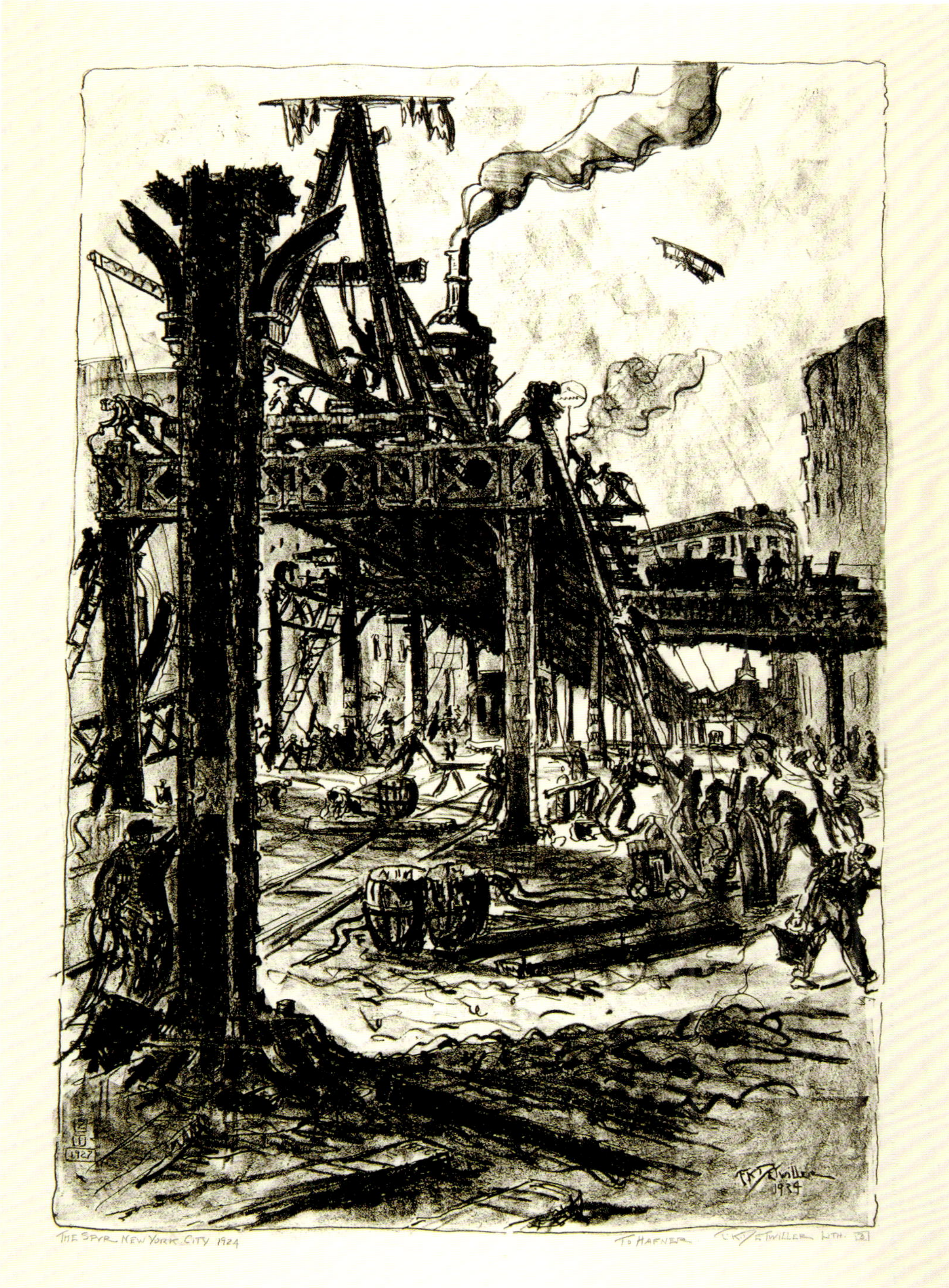

16. Frederick K. Detwiller: *The Spur, New York City*, 1924; lithograph. Catalogue no. 56

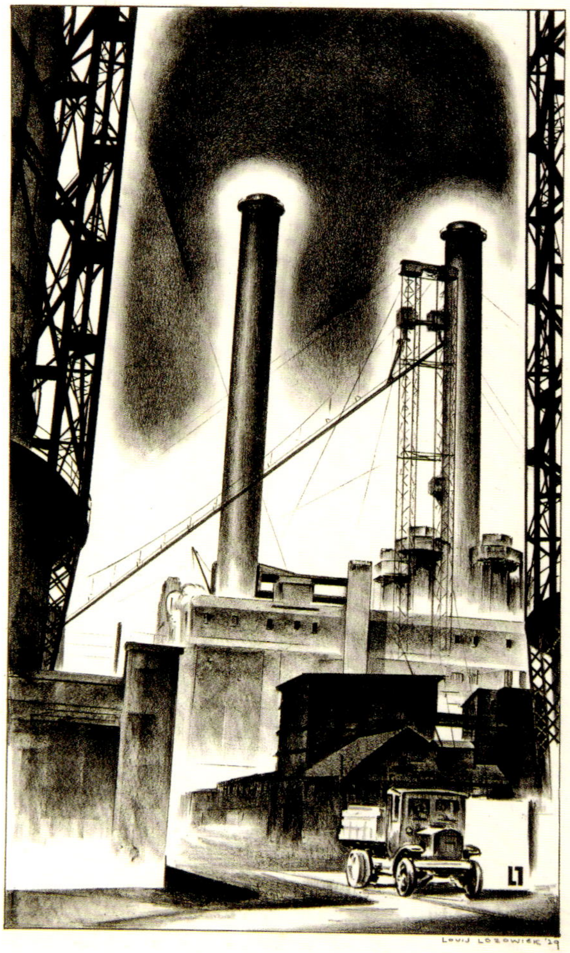

17. Louis Lozowick: *Edison Plant*, 1929; lithograph. Catalogue no. 30

of one away to free the street below from noise and shadow was more a sign of progress than the construction of a new line would have been. A generation younger than Pennell, Detwiller uses a more vigorous line. His heavy shading accentuates the darkness of the old ironwork and its contrast to the light falling on the newly cleared street. The low viewpoint and abrupt perspective of his image makes the old line

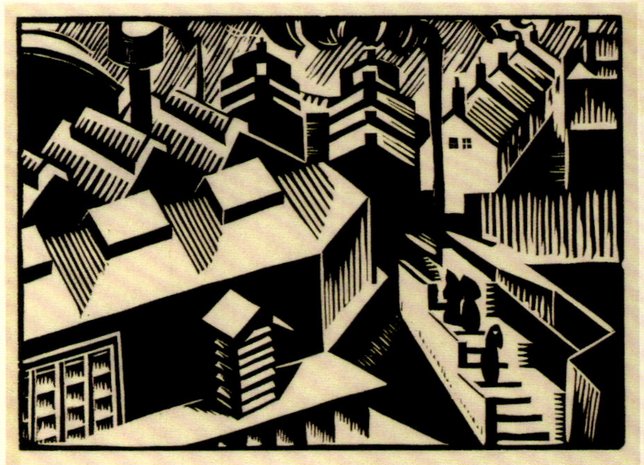

18. Edward Wadsworth: *Yorkshire*, 1920; woodcut. Catalogue no. 70.

appear to swoop towards us, and one suspects that he may have introduced the airplane in the sky above (probably still a fairly rare sight in 1924) as a metaphor: the high-flying plane above the low-flying train. Like the airplane, the puffing smoke from the steam crane draws our eyes upward from the shadowed underside of the El into a light-filled sky.

A few years later than Detwiller, Louis Lozowick depicted mechanical power in a very different way. In *Edison Plant* (fig.17) the image itself seems to be machine-made. Aptly nicknamed "Precisionism," Lozowick's style idealizes the machine as an academic artist might idealize the human body. If for Pennell and Detwiller industry is King Kong, for Lozowick it is the Apollo Belvedere. It is noteworthy that Lozowick's smokestacks, unlike Pennell's or Detwiller's, do not belch smoke. It is not clear whether this is a plant that actually burns a cleaner fuel, or is still under construction, or has simply been idealized. However, as a plant presumably intended to produce the clean energy of electricity, its smokeless appearance is appropriate, whether accurate or not. Instead of smoke belching from their tops, the stacks are surrounded by halos of white.

Edward Wadsworth uses a modernist style as clean-cut as Lozowick's to give a more ambiguous view of the urban industrial environment. Wadsworth was one of the first British artists to welcome the new styles of the early twentieth century: Cubism and Futurism. At the time of *Yorkshire* (fig.18) he had recently completed service with the British army in the First World War and was dealing with what his friend Paul Nash called "the struggle of a war artist without a war." In 1919 he had produced a series of prints and drawings of slag heaps and other industrial wastelands in the "black country" of Staffordshire in central England. This is one of several prints made the following year and associated with the northern region of Yorkshire.

The print's style combines order with agitation. The landscape is reduced to patches of black and white, defining sharp-edged prisms, but instead of a crystalline calm there is a restless instability in the X-like composition with few vertical lines and fewer horizontals. The print has the elegant generalization of a sheet of labor statistics. Even the figures ascending the stepped street at the right are reduced to angular shapes. The title gives no clue as to which of the various Yorkshire industrial areas Wadsworth is representing, but Wadsworth had grown up in the Yorkshire town of Cleckheaton, where his family owned a textile mill, and the generic title of the print may conceal a reference to his own roots. The mills and domestic housing with a stepped street between convey the image of a small mill town on a hillside, but it is an image that invites intellectual rather than emotional understanding. If there is any political message here it is distanced and neutral, neither glorifying the orderly buildings nor inviting sympathy for the diminutive figures.

If the prints of Luce, Pennell, Detwiller, and Lozowick define a heroic industrial landscape, an equally heroic presentation of the worker appears in a variety of prints from the nineteenth and twentieth centuries. The nature of the heroism varies with the political stance of the artist.

19. Compagnie Française des papiers-monnaie: *J. and O. G. Pierson, calendar for 1896*, 1895: engraving. Catalogue no. 49

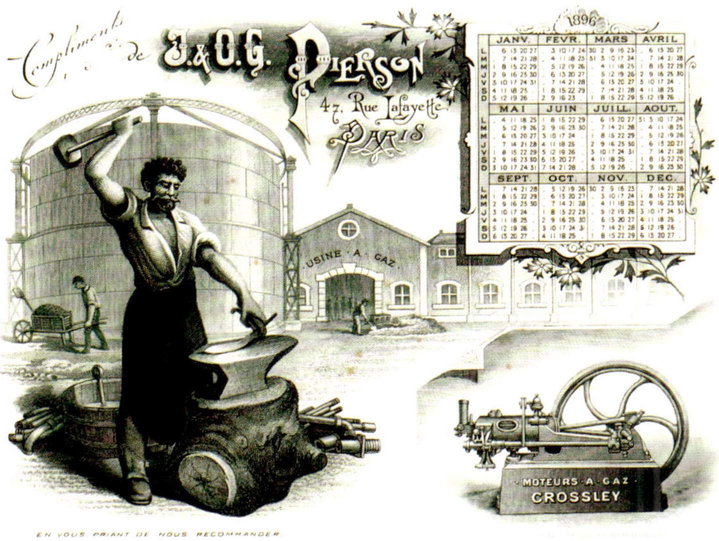

At the conservative end of the spectrum is an 1896 calendar (fig.19) for the Pierson Company, which evidently specialized in the production of coal-gas and marketing of gas-powered engines, a novelty in the 1890s. But the one prominent human figure is a blacksmith, beating out his iron on an anvil that sits on a barely trimmed log. As a transitional figure between the preindustrial and the industrial age, the blacksmith had been a primary emblem of labor in the early nineteenth century, but by 1896 such an image verged on the archaic. For the management and the customers of the Pierson Company, this solitary craftsman would have been well-calculated to turn their attention away from the actual labor force of the time, with threats of labor unrest, unions, and strikes. It is appropriate that the style and technique of the print is equally archaic; a form of engraving that by the 1890s was seldom used except for currency, postage stamps, and stock certificates.

20. Théophile Steinlen: *The Last Refuge of Liberty*, 1894; lithograph. Catalogue no. 66

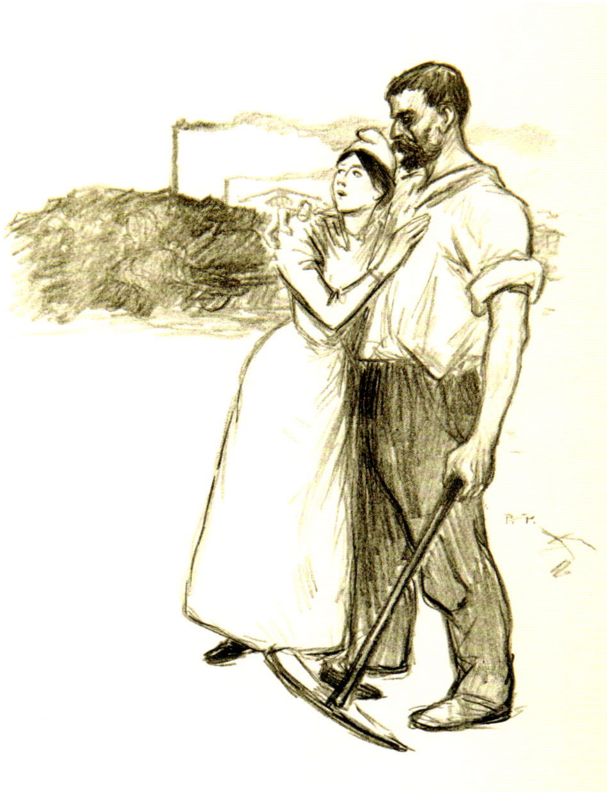

At the opposite extreme is Steinlen's lithograph (fig.20) for a socialist newspaper, *Le Chambard socialiste* (The Socialist Rumpus). The woman in this print is identified as Liberty, but by her appearance and costume she could equally well represent Marianne, the personification of the French republic as Uncle Sam is of the United States. Liberty's last refuge is the worker, symbolized by a miner (the background, behind a mound of coal, shows what is probably a mine building). The miner's labor was hardly more mechanized than the blacksmith's, but unlike the blacksmith miners worked in vast armies. Mining was not only unpleasant but one of the most dangerous kinds of labor – as indeed it still is. Beneath the peaceful landscapes that Bonhommé depicted at Blanzy (fig.9; Catalogue no. 8-10) there were nine mine disasters in the five decades between 1850 and 1900, with a total of 231 victims.

In both Europe and America the indifference of mine-owners to the miners' condition made the mines a fertile ground for union organization, and by the end of the century the voracious appetite of industrial civilization for coal automatically made a miners' strike a social crisis. Zola's novel *Germinal*, centered on an unsuccessful strike, presents a society that will be destroyed by the conflict between uncaring mine owners and desperate miners, but its end offers a ray of hope for a better future. *Germinal* had been successful both in its original form and as a

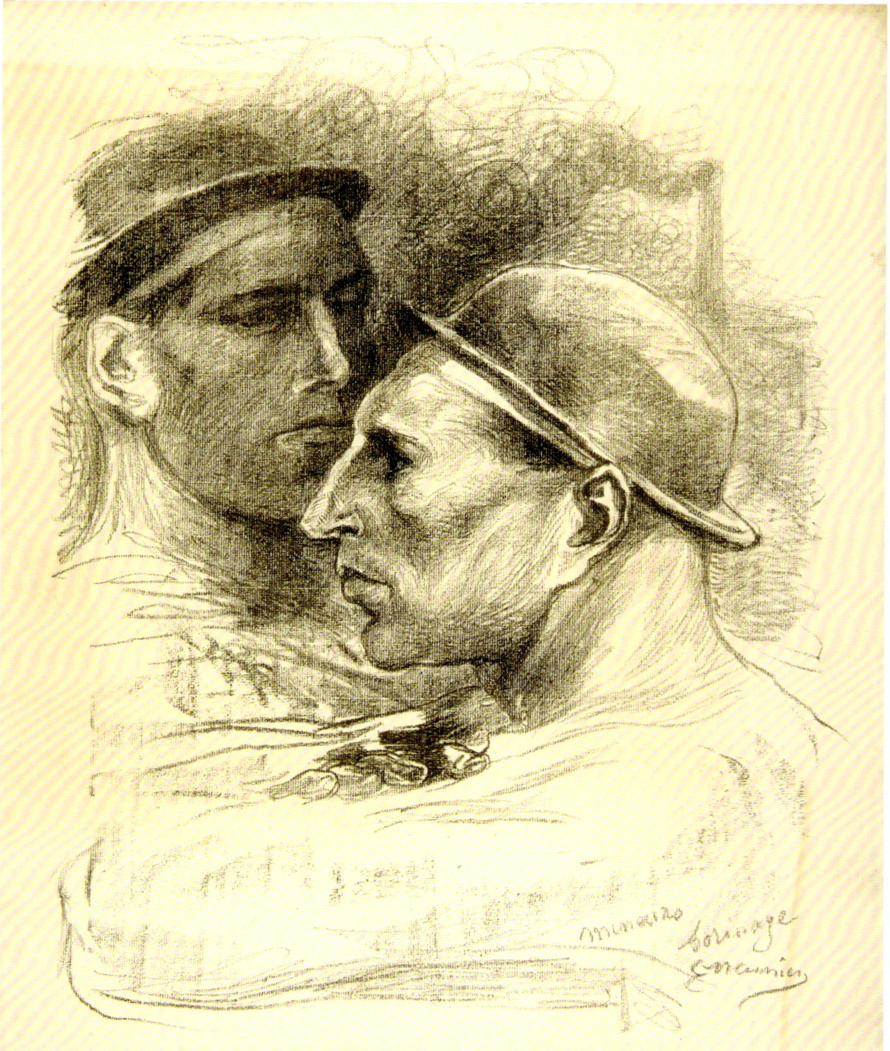

21. Constantin Meunier: *Miners, Borinage*, 1898; lithograph. Catalogue no. 22

play, and this, in addition to actual strikes, must have made the miner a logical personification of labor as an organized force for change.

Steinlen's use of technical processes was as timely as his imagery. The print in this exhibition is a lithograph aimed at print collectors, but on the cover of *Le Chambard socialiste* it appeared as a photomechanical reproduction, colored by stencil: a mass-produced object suited to mass communication.

Constantin Meunier's lithograph of miners from the Borinage coal fields in Belgium (fig.21) offers a still more potent image of labor. Meunier had worked for years as a painter when a trip in 1881 to the Borinage region, also known as *le pays noir* (the black country), convinced him to choose sculpture as a medium and labor as a subject. By the 1890s he was recognized as the preeminent artist of the worker, and in 1916 he was acclaimed by Pennell as "the prophet and exponent of the Wonder of Work." To some Meunier's sculpture offered a reassuring portrayal of laborers devoted to their work, inured to suffering and too weary to revolt. It is noteworthy that in 1914 the millionaire George W. Vanderbilt purchased eight pieces to adorn his colossal mansion, Biltmore, in the North Carolina mountains.

This lithograph, however, published by the anarchist journal *Les Temps nouveaux* (The New Era), portrays two miners in an attitude that is far from submissive. Their fully modeled heads rise from barely sketched lines that indicate arms and shoulders but

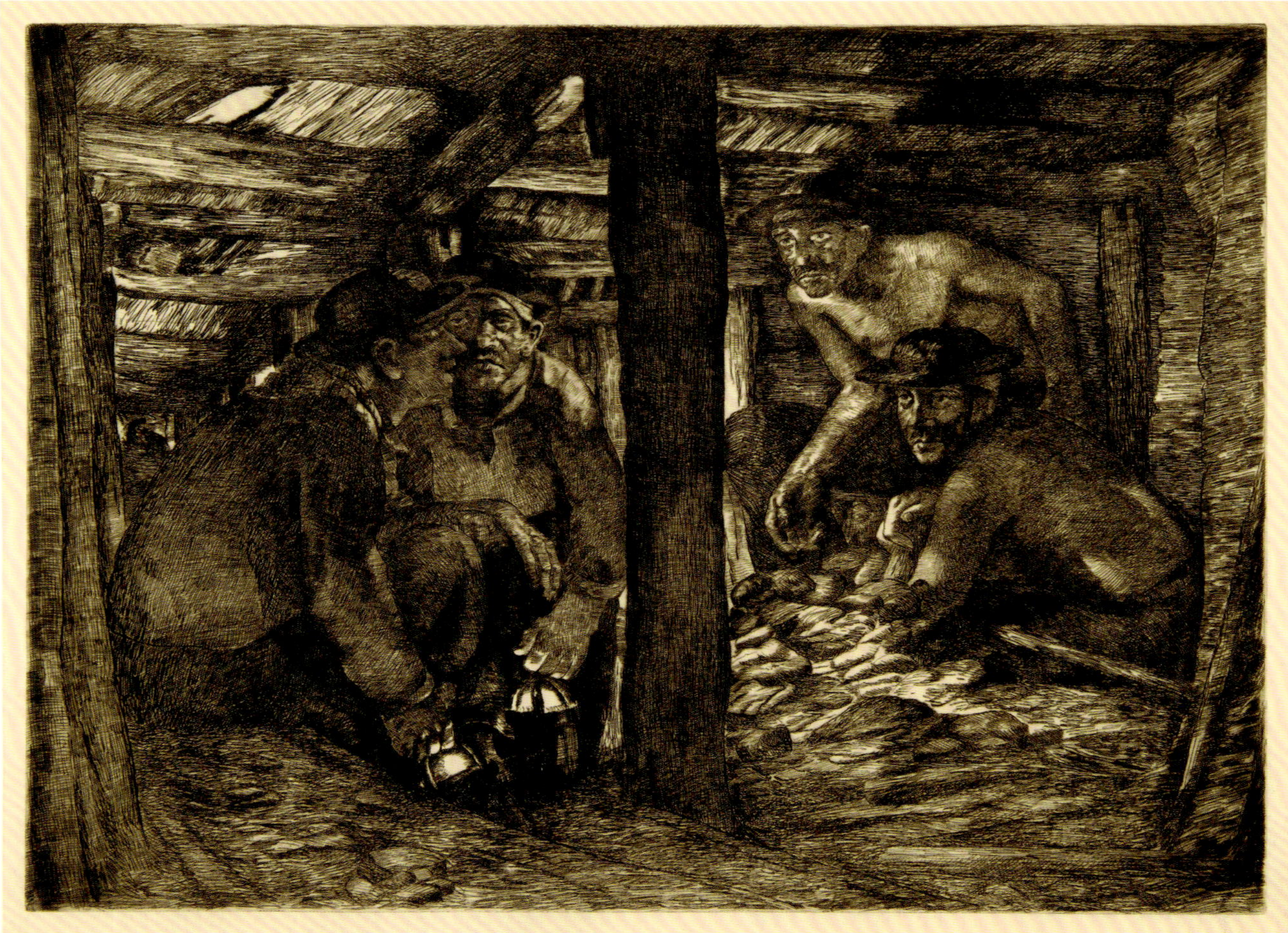

22. Gustave Pierre: *Miners at rest, Underground*, 1937; etching. Catalogue no. 23

could be read as the hills and valleys of a landscape – nearly life size on the paper, they become colossal in our imagination as the presidents on Mount Rushmore. At the same time the profile of the man in the foreground calls to mind the profiles of kings and heroes on coins and medals. Looking either straight ahead or slightly upwards, the two men seem neither to acknowledge nor to avoid the viewer. What may seem their military appearance is an illusion – in 1897 soldiers had yet to adopt helmets that would resemble the miners' protective leather caps – but they convey immense strength and potential for action. Ironically another portrayal of miners from the Borinage, nearly forty years later, seems to present just the sort of passive image that Meunier rejected. Gustave Pierre's etching (fig.22) is part of a portfolio issued by the management of the Henzies-Pommeroeul coal mines to celebrate the twenty-fifth anniversary of the firm. As a corporate celebration the portfolio is remarkably grim; neither in this etching nor in the others is there any sign of happiness or enthusiasm among the workers. It is tempting to think that Pierre was playing a practical joke on his patrons, but more likely he was making the best of an impossible commission. Five years earlier a powerful documentary film about the wretchedness of life in the Belgian mines, *Misère au Borinage* (Extreme Poverty in the Borinage district), had won international acclaim. It may be that these exhausted men, crouched in a tunnel where they cannot stand upright, were as positive an image as Pierre could present without straining credulity. The juxtaposition of profile and full-face in the two miners at the left is probably a coincidence, but makes a bitterly ironic comparison to Meunier's lithograph.

Historically, Pierre's image is separated from Meunier's by the catastrophes of war and economic depression. From 1914 to 1918 the industrial giants of Europe, eventually joined by the United States, fought against each other with unprecedented, inhuman mechanical power. In 1917 H. G. Wells, whose early science-fiction novels were already being outdated by technological progress, introduced a book by Pennell depicting war-related industry in England. He praised Pennell for neglecting the battlefield in favor of "the huge industrial apparatus that is thrusting up through the war of the gentlemen in spurs" and declared: "War by these developments has become the monopoly of the five great industrial powers."[12] Considering the mechanization of warfare it is not surprising that the World

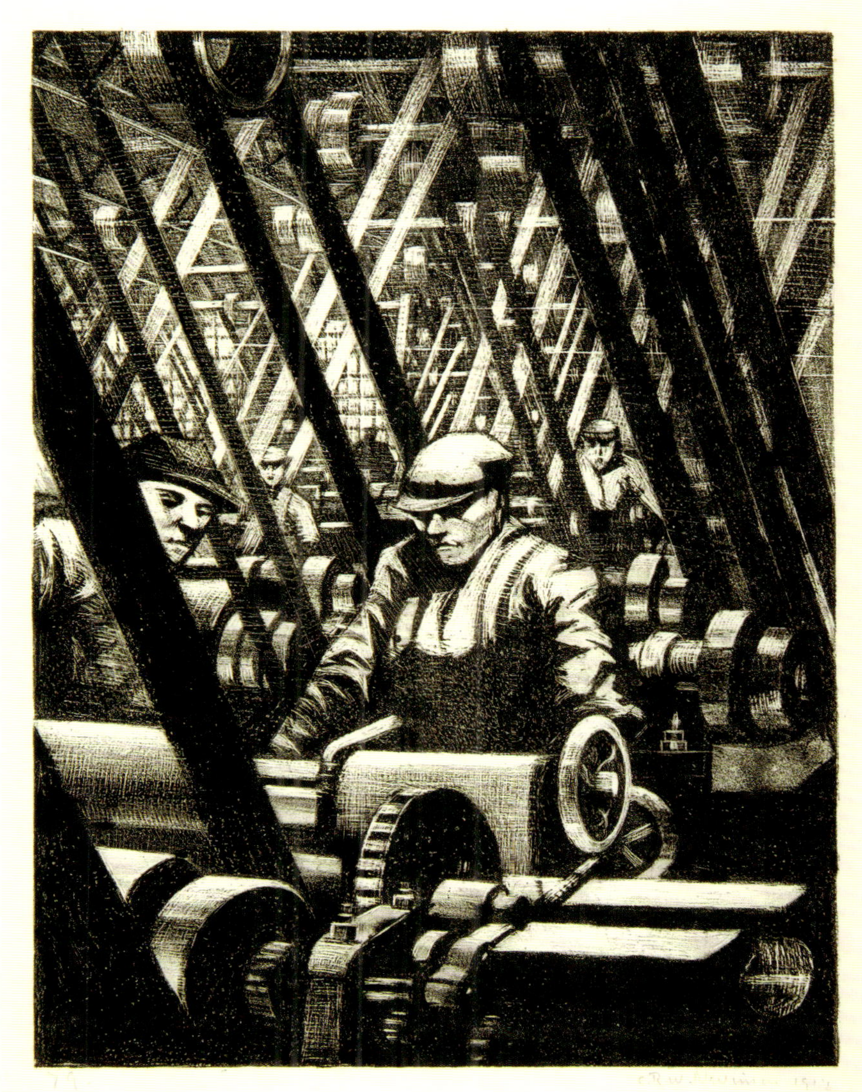

23. C. R. W. Nevinson: *Making the Engine*, 1917; lithograph. Catalogue no. 55

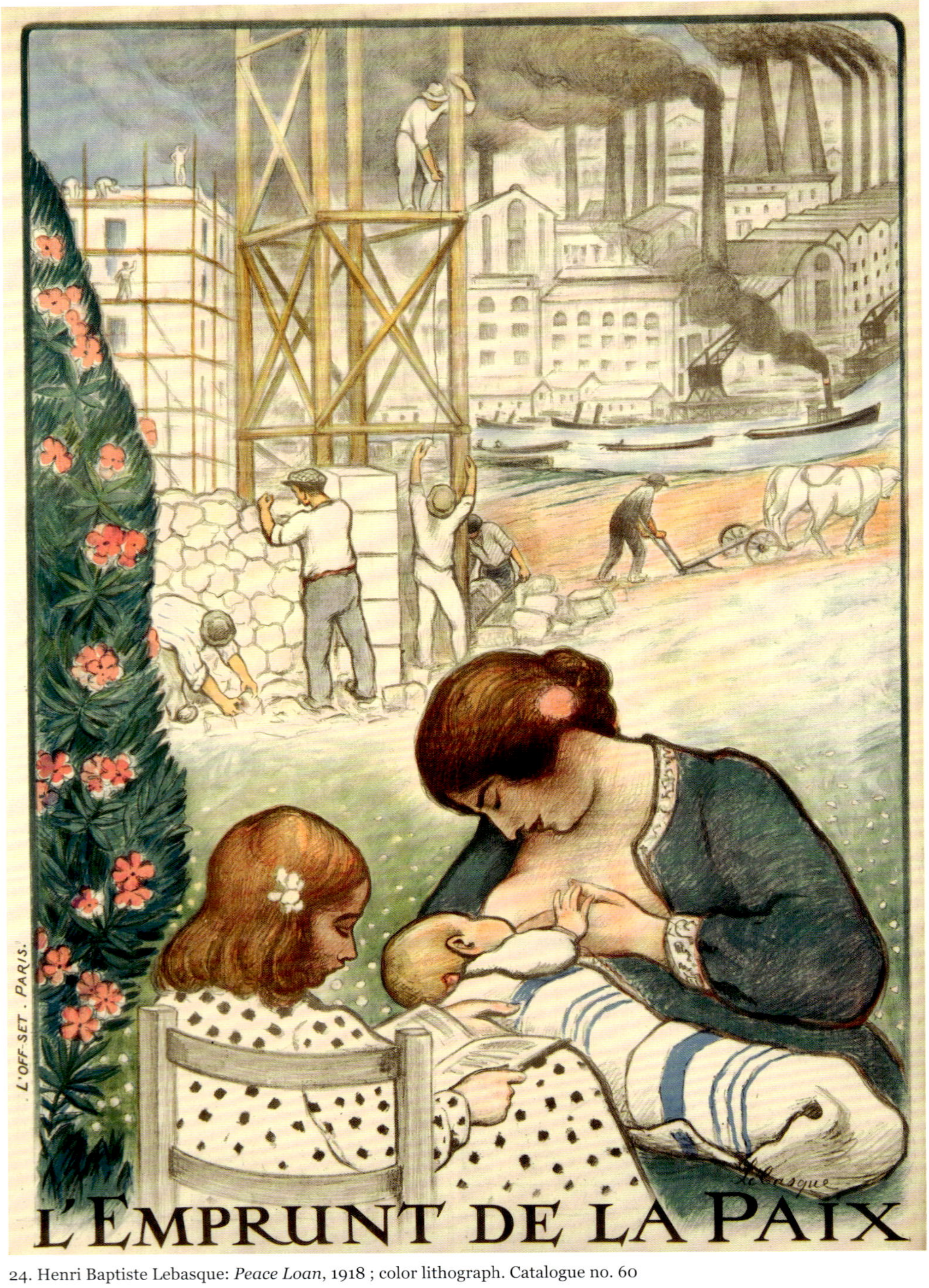

24. Henri Baptiste Lebasque: *Peace Loan*, 1918 ; color lithograph. Catalogue no. 60

War and its aftermath gave rise to a whole range of industrial imagery in posters and other forms, as each nation called on its civilian population to support the war effort. C. R. W. Nevinson's lithograph (fig.23) comes from a series of patriotic prints by numerous artists issued under the title "Britain's Aims and Ideals in the War." Like his friend Wadsworth, Nevinson was influenced by Cubism and Futurism, particularly the worship of speed and machinery promulgated by the Italian Futurists. His expressionless machinists, embedded in the factory environment, are nearly as impersonal as the figures in Wadsworth's print (fig.18). The real excitement of the composition comes from the crystalline masses of machinery and the dynamic pattern of intersecting power belts that fill the background. Ironically, Nevinson's futurism is belied by the machinery he depicts. Airplanes might be at the cutting edge of technology in 1917, but a factory where power was transmitted by belts and pulleys rather than electricity was not. The belt-driven machine shop, which also appears in Pennell's lithographs of war work in England, is one sign that in the early twentieth century British industry had lost its early lead and was falling behind.

In the aftermath of the catastrophic war, mixtures of traditional and contemporary labor could have a deliberate purpose: reassuring the viewer that ordinary life had survived. A French poster by Henri Lebasque from the final year of the war (fig.24) invites subscriptions to a "Peace Loan," presumably a government bond issue, to provide for reconstruction. Lebasque gives us a progression from intimate to industrial, with each element carefully calculated. Beside a blooming oleander bush, a mother nurses her baby: significantly, in a nation concerned about its falling birthrate, this is her second child. Behind the domestic scene masons construct a wall of irregular stone, and a farmer guides a one-horse plow, while further back a

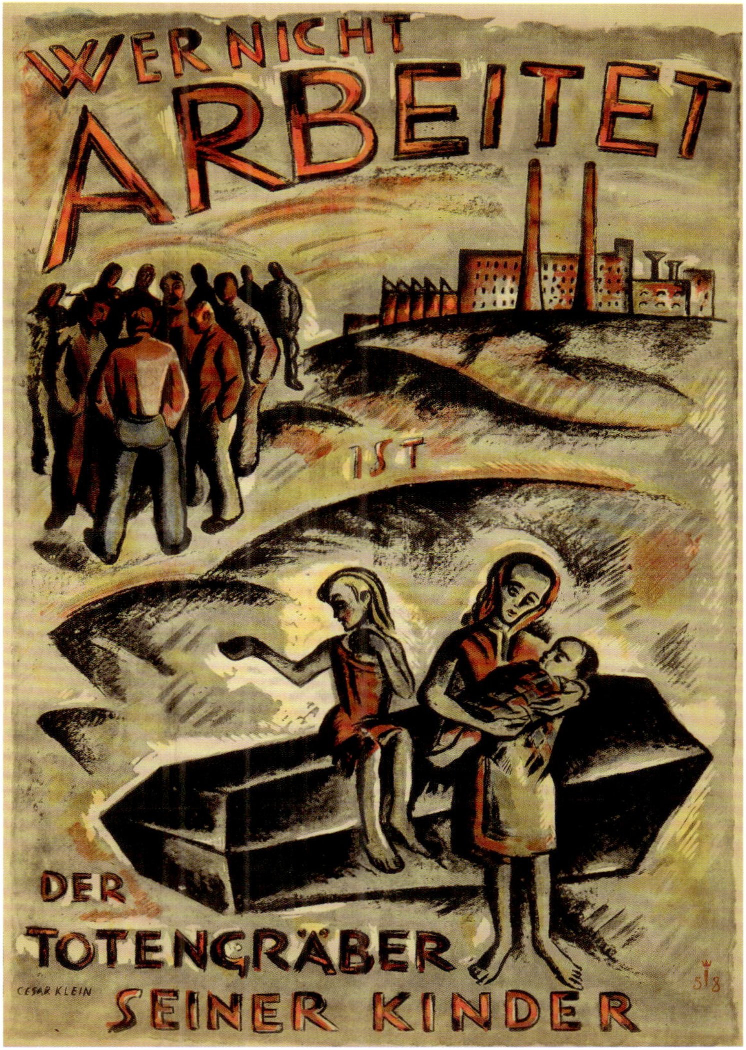

25. Cesar Klein: *The One Who Does not Work is his Children's Gravedigger*, 1919; color lithograph. Catalogue no. 61. © Artists Rights Society (ARS), New York / VG Bild-Kunst, Bonn

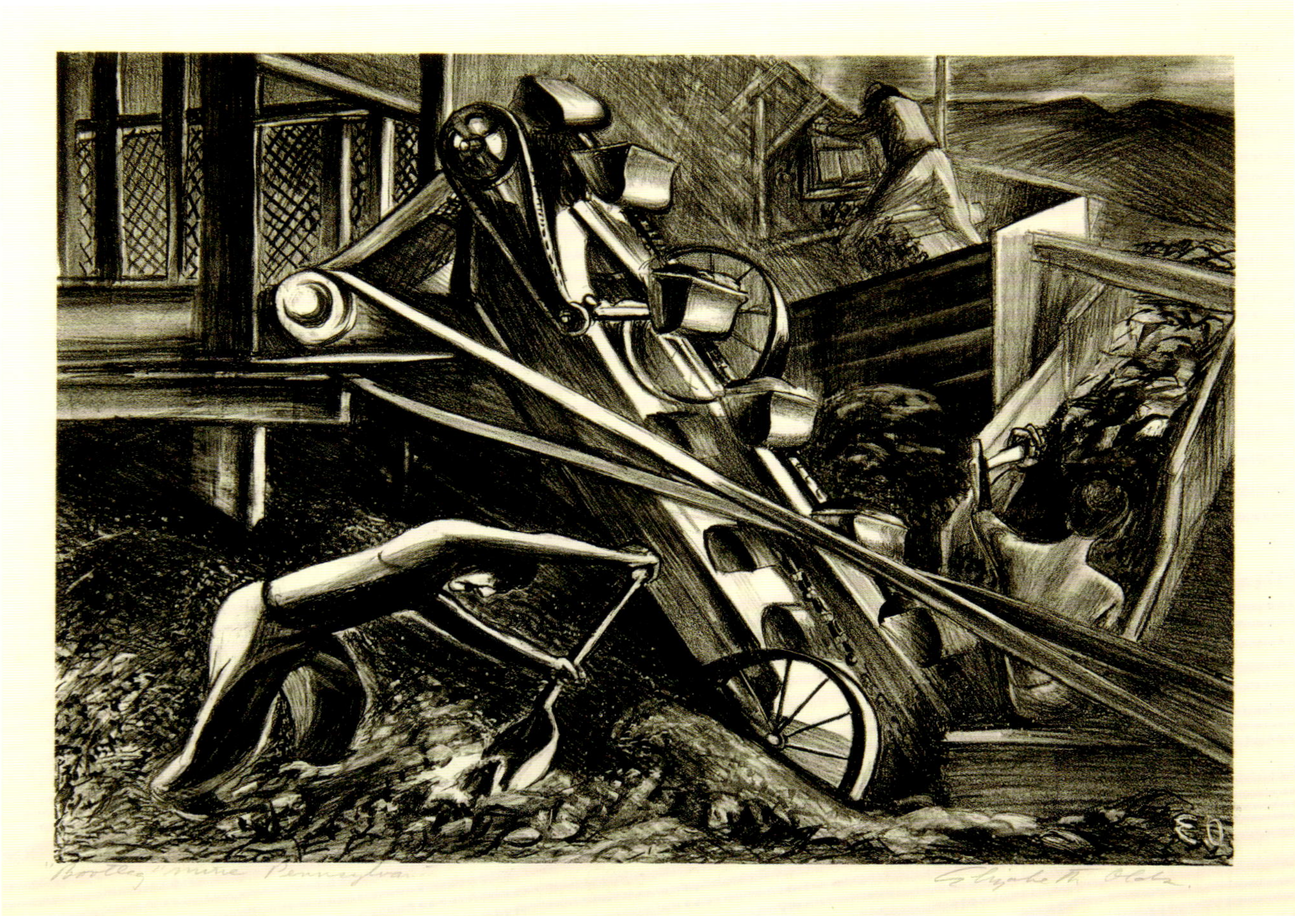

26. Elizabeth Olds: *"Bootleg" Mine, Pennsylvania*, 1937; lithograph. Catalogue no. 12

multistory building rises, and beyond a river filled with shipping, a city of factories stretches across the horizon. Overall, the poster can be seen as the invocation of a hoped-for fecundity, with the factory chimneys a technological equivalent to the mother's flowing breast. Although they fill the air with smoke, they conveniently leave a significant patch of blue sky.

A German poster from the following year by Cesar Klein (fig.25) suggests a drastic difference in attitude between France and Germany at the end of the war. Having replaced the discredited imperial German regime in November 1918, a provisional socialist government faced the formidable task of "nation-building" in the face of military defeat and without any national consensus among communists, liberals, monarchists, and other factions. Klein was a co-founder of the *Novembergruppe* (November Group), an organization of avant-garde artists and architects formed to support the provisional republic, which would not acquire a constitution until mid-1919. The politics of the *Novembergruppe* artists were generally left-wing, but more idealist than Marxist in orientation. Klein's poster is one of several he created for the new government in the Expressionist style pioneered by several groups of German artists before the war.

In contrast to Lebasque's contented family group, Klein gives us three malnourished children standing before a coffin (their mother's?). Further back a crowd of men face each other in apparent discussion, while in the distance a factory stands with smokeless chimneys. The first impression, particularly if we associate German Expressionism with left-wing politics, is that this is a scene of economic crisis and unemployment. But studying the image more closely reveals the meaning of the grim caption: "The One who does not Work is his Children's Gravedigger." Not the one who cannot get work, but the one who does not work because he is on strike. The appeal is not to the government or the factory owner but to the worker, to support the new government through a time of crisis before making his own demands.

Klein's intense color and effectively simplified forms produce an intense and striking image: the engaged yet inconclusive discussion of the men and the passive suffering of the emaciated children are powerfully conveyed. Yet it is hardly surprising that posters like these were ineffective in rallying workers to the new republic. The modernism of the *Novembergruppe* artists alienated workers, who perceived their expressive distortion as caricature. Although the group persisted as an artists' organization, its political activism rapidly faded. When Hitler's government banned the group in 1933 it was not for political activity, but because the Nazis saw modernist styles as inherently suspect politically.

In a final irony, the Nazi condemnation of Expressionism as a style probably helped it gain popularity in progressive circles outside Germany, particularly in America. The work of Elizabeth Olds combines an expressive distortion that derives, at least indirectly, from German Expressionism, with a humorous caricature that almost certainly does not. Like many printmakers active during the Depression of the 1930s, Olds mixed satire, documentation, and social protest in varying proportions. *"Bootleg" Mine, Pennsylvania* (fig.26) depicts an activity described in 1935 by the writer Louis Adamic as "one of the most

27. Robert Martin: *Coal Pickers*, 1940; lithograph. Catalogue no. 32.

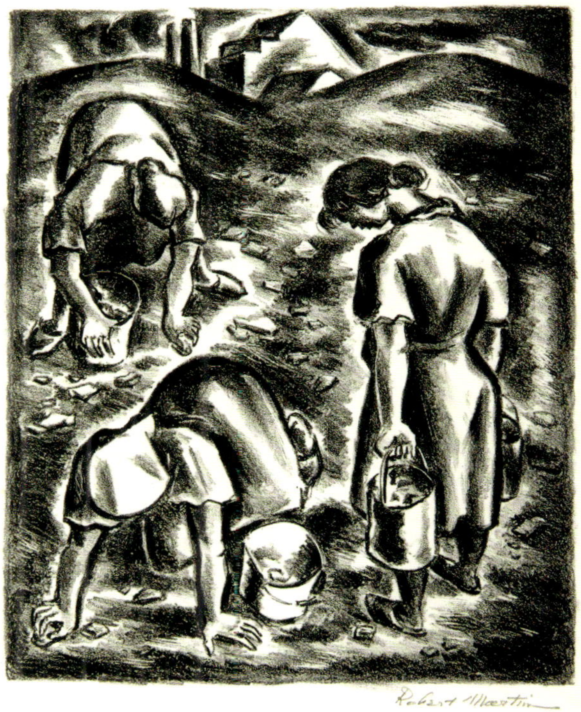

interesting, not to say exciting, socioeconomic phenomena developed in the United States during these years of depression – the so-called 'bootleg' coal, coal illegally mined by the unemployed in the mining towns from company-owned lands, for the most part in open daylight, by the most primitive methods imaginable, in complete disregard of private property rights and successful defiance of company police, and, in most places, with the full approval of the constituted authorities and of the overwhelming majority of the other inhabitants of the community…"[13] According to Adamic the practice had begun with men mining a few buckets of coal for their own use and under depression conditions had grown to a small-scale industry. The danger of the operations, the small profits they yielded, and the degree to which those profits benefited the community led him to portray it as a kind of Robin Hood activity. Olds shows the aboveground phase of this kind of mining, breaking up and sorting the coal with some primitive equipment. The unstable composition and confusing spatial relationships accentuate the improvised nature of the mining. She draws the miner in the foreground with a casual freedom that verges on caricature, but at least to an outsider the humor seems sympathetic rather than condescending.

Robert Martin's *Coal Pickers* (fig.27) depicts a still more marginal form of coal gathering: gleaning coal from waste dumps for family use. In a slightly stylized realism Martin depicts three women, strong but worn and bent, in this arduous scavenging. With none of Olds' humor, his aim would seem to be akin to the documentary photography of his time, presenting a subject without idealization but with a kind of dignity.

The prints by Olds and Martin represent only a minute sample of the vast number of 1930s American prints dealing with labor and industry. Government programs like the Federal Art Project were supplemented by initiatives taken by artists themselves in the hope that a middle-class, and perhaps even a working-class, public could be interested in these relatively inexpensive works of art. In the following decades several factors combined to diminish this production. Various forms of abstraction displaced the realist and expressionist styles that had been congenial to the imagery. Prints themselves went out of fashion for a while among artists and collectors. Photography, which had been competing with printmaking as a means of documenting industry since the late nineteenth century, finally gained general recognition as an independent art form, and as the medium of choice for representing the world. Finally, by the 1970s and 1980s when a variety of realist styles re-emerged in painting and printmaking, the great mines, mills, and factories themselves were very different from what they had been. One of the great migrations of history was taking place in the last quarter of the twentieth century: the migration of heavy industry from Europe and America to other parts of the globe. In the depiction of great industrial sites, the late twentieth century gave birth to a new romanticism, a kind of mirror image of the wonder with which pioneers like Loutherbourg had brought to it at the beginning of the Industrial Revolution. The final prints in this exhibition have an elegiac tone.

Craig McPherson has said that he sees his work as "history paintings … documenting the remnants of our Industrial Age."[14] His print *Clairton* (fig.28) looks backward in several ways. First, the medium, mezzotint, is a laborious preindustrial handicraft: the artist systematically roughens the entire surface of a copper plate so that it will trap ink, and then creates an image by selectively polishing parts of the plate to produce highlights. It was used extensively in the eighteenth century to reproduce paintings: in fact the eighteenth-century mezzotints resulted not only from a division of labor between designer and printmaker, but the printmaker himself delegated the laborious roughening of the plate to apprentices. McPherson, by contrast, conscientiously practices every step of the process himself, from preliminary drawing to preparation of the plate to printed edition. Second, the subject is a mill that processes coal into coke, the same process that had helped to start the Industrial Revolution in Coalbrookdale two centuries earlier.

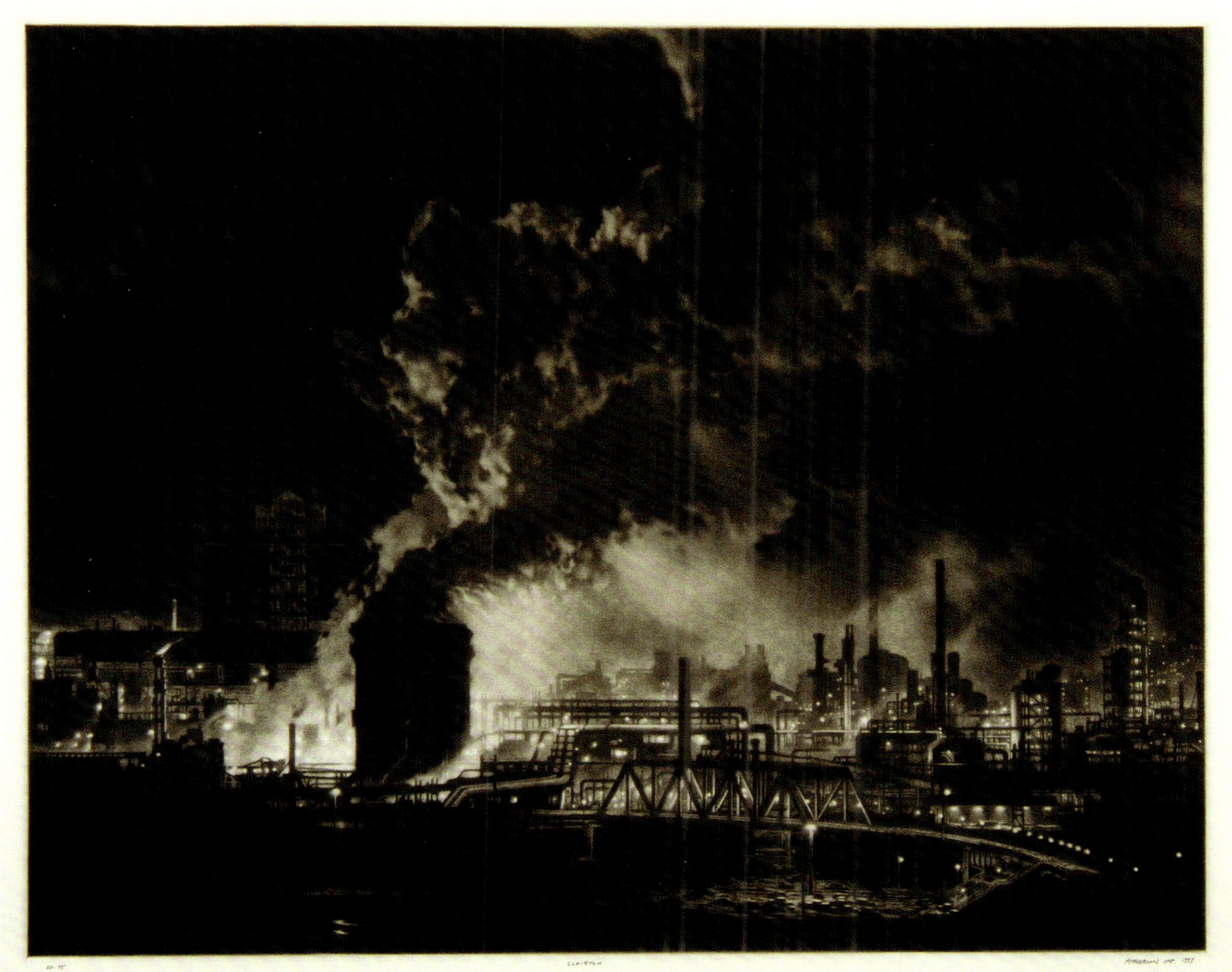

28. Craig McPherson: *Clairton*, 1997; mezzotint on green paper. Catalogue no. 76

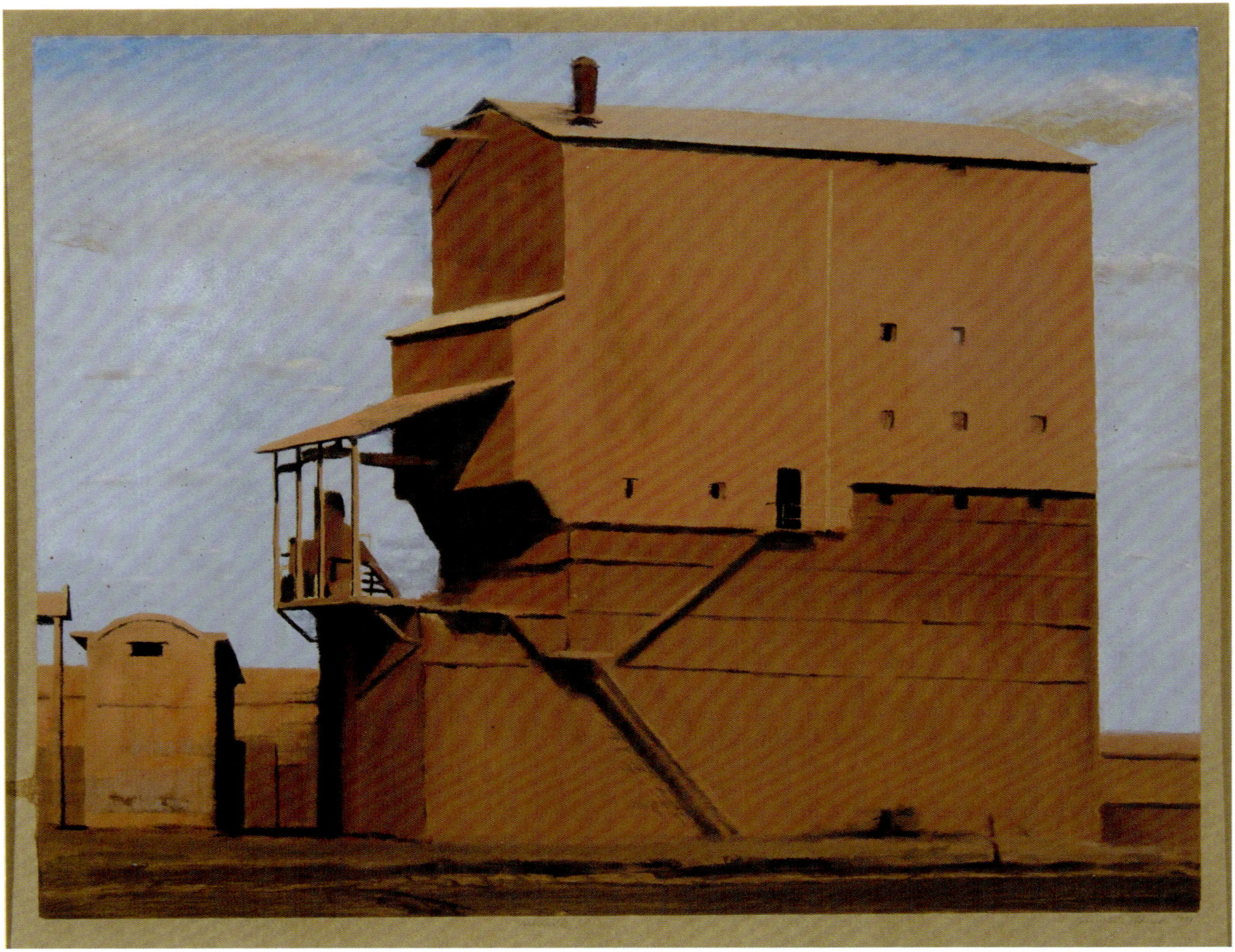

29. Jean-Baptiste Secheret: *Mondeville*, 1991; color monotype on brown paper. Catalogue no. 74. © 2009 Artists Rights Society (ARS), New York/ADAGP, Paris

Like several of the earliest artists to depict industry, McPherson emphasizes the volcanic appearance of fire in the night. Finally, in depicting a vast plant that fills the plate, he recreates Pennell's world of gigantic, triumphant industry. But we cannot look at this view with the eyes of those who first viewed Pennell's prints. Seeing the billowing smoke, the first thought that comes to mind is "pollution," not "power" or "prosperity," and we are also aware that this plant is a survivor within a declining industry. Because McPherson has used a greenish paper, even the glowing highlights of the print have a cool, melancholy color.

As for Europe, most of the great industrial sites represented in this catalogue have vanished over the past fifty years. Coalbrookdale is a complex of museums, documenting early industry. Mining has ceased at Blanzy and in the Borinage. Steel-making continues in Sheffield and Le Creusot, but they are no longer the major industrial centers they once were. The *Société métallurgique de Normandie*, a great steel works in the French town of Mondeville during most of the twentieth century, was shutting down in the early 1990s when Jean-Baptiste Secheret made a series of views there. In contrast to McPherson's active mill, the building in *Mondeville* (fig.29) radiates abandonment, even though it shows no sign of decay. The flat coloring and simplification suggest the industrial precisionism of Lozowick's Edison plant, but the iron-red surfaces are weightier and not so hard-edged as Lozowick's, as if they had become a little worn. There is no obvious clue to the building's function, and no human presence, and this leads to the disturbing difficulty of establishing its scale. At first the open structure on the left side seems to have the homely feel of a front porch; then we notice the much smaller door to the right. Do we measure a human scale by the door, the even smaller windows, or by the zig-zag external staircase (if that indeed is what it is)? Each new measure makes the structure larger. Yet this vast structure is obviously only one part of a much larger complex that extends behind it to the left and right. Other buildings block our view of anything but the sky with its drifting clouds, and it seems almost as if one of those clouds might pass in front of this colossus instead of behind it. In its giant size and its palpable lack of activity the building has an air of stoic desolation, even greater than if it were actually being demolished or falling into picturesque ruin.

* * *

Should we look at images like McPherson's and Secheret's as elegies for industrial civilization? That would surely be premature. The era of roaring fires and belching smokestacks is coming to an end, but worldwide industry is not dead, or even dying. Coal and iron may share the throne with oil, aluminum, and silicon, and steam power may be largely invisible in the depths of the electric generating plant, but the old trinity is still here. The "post-industrial" civilization of Europe and America owes its existence to industrial development on other continents. China, which now produces five times as much steel as the United States, is undergoing its own industrial revolution, and so are other nations in Asia and elsewhere.

Of course there are graver threats to industrial civilization than the mere migration of an industry from one continent to another. Pollution ignores national boundaries. Over the last two decades scientific evidence for climate change, and for our own role in that change, has gradually become irrefutable. The struggle to preserve a habitable earth in the twenty-first century may dwarf the world wars of the twentieth. But this will be a very different kind of struggle from those wars: fundamentally we are all on the same side this time, though like most allies we will surely quarrel bitterly among ourselves.

I began this essay by saying that it was not a history of the Industrial Revolution, and it would be reckless to conclude with a prophetic history of its next phase. But hope is not reckless, as long as we realize that hope is only a beginning. Let us hope, then, that just as the industry of wooden looms and waterpower was a prelude to the era of coal, iron, and steam, so that era may be the prelude to a new era, when active industry no longer generates the fire and smoke of McPherson's *Clairton*, and where the clear skies above Secheret's *Mondeville* no longer imply an industry in decay. Let us hope for a metamorphosis of industry into something very different from what we have known over the last two centuries. Yet whatever form that new industrial civilization takes, and whatever artistic representations document it, it will be a continuation and a result of the industry depicted in this exhibition.

NOTES

1. Quoted (without source) by M. Ross, "Preliminary Observations" in Thomas Hair, *The Mines of Durham and Northumbria*, (London:James Madden and Co. and T. H. Hair, 1844), 1.

2. T. K. Derry and Trevor I. Williams, *A Short History of Technology* (Oxford: Oxford University Press, 1961), 478.

3. David Landes, *The Unbound Prometheus* (Cambridge: Cambridge University Press, 1969), 218.

4. Thomas Hair, *The Mines of Durham and Northumbria*, (London:James Madden and Co. and T. H. Hair, 1844), iii.

5. The title of the print in the exhibition refers to the *département* of Saône-et-Loire, one of the administrative regions created by the French Revolutionary government in 1791, but the view does not include the glass works constructed beyond the foundry in 1786. An earlier version of the same image (probably an earlier state of the print) describes it as the "Royal Foundry" in the province of Burgundy.

6. *Punch*, XXVI (25 February 1854) 82. Reprinted in *John Leech's Pictures of Life and Character; from the Collection of 'Mr. Punch'* I (London: Bradbury, Agnew and Co., n.d.) 121.

7. Quoted in *La Représentation du travail: mines, forges, usines*: [exhibition catalogue] (Le Creuzot: Château de la Verrerie, septembre 1977 - février 1978), 17.

8. Cited in Robyn Roslak, *Neo-impressionism and anarchism in fin-de-siècle France: painting, politics and landscape* (Aldershot, England; Burlington, VT: Ashgate Pub., c. 2007), 105.

9. Toute la mer va vers la ville!

Son port est pluvieux de suie à travers brumes
Où le soleil comme un oeil rouge et colossal larmoie.

Son port est ameuté de steamers qui fument
Et mugissent, au fond du soir, sans qu'on les voie.
Emile Verhaeren, "Le Port" in *Les villes tentaculaires* in *Œuvres*, II (Genève: Slatkine Reprints, 1977), 127-28. Translation by T. Riggs.

10. Rectangles de granit et monuments de briques,
Et longs murs noirs durant des lieues
Immensément, par les banlieues;
Et sur les toits, dans le brouillard, aiguillonées
De fers et de paratonnerres,
Les cheminées.
"Les Usines" in *Les villes tentaculaires* in *Œuvres*, II (Genève: Slatkine Reprints, 1977), 145-46. Translation by T. Riggs.

11. Joseph Pennell, *Joseph Pennell's Pictures of the Wonder of Work* (Philadelphia and London: J. B. Lippincott, 1916), Pl. XXXVI, "The Great Stack, Sheffield."

12. Preface to *Joseph Pennell's Pictures of War Work in England* (Philadelphia: J. B. Lippincott; London: William Heinemann, 1917), vi.

13. Louis Adamic, "The Great 'Bootleg' Coal Industry," *The Nation*, 140 (January 9, 1935), 46.

14. Sarah J. Hall, "A conversation with Craig McPherson" in *Steel: Pittsburg Drawings by Craig McPherson* (Pittsburgh: Frick Art and Historical Center, 2008), [unpaginated].

Select Bibliography

The following bibliography is limited to books that provided essential factual information for the catalogue essay or that shaped its point of view. Additional sources for material directly quoted in the essay are found in the Notes.

GENERAL

T. K. Derry and Trevor I. Williams, *A Short History of Technology from the Earliest Times to A.D. 1900.* (New York: Oxford University Press, 1961).

E. J. Hobsbawm and C.Wrigley, *Industry and Empire: from 1750 to the present day.* (New York: New Press, 1999).

Francis d. Klingender, *Art and the Industrial Revolution* (edited and revised by Arthur Elton) (New York: Schocken books, 1970).

David S. Landes, *The Unbound Prometheus: Technological change and industrial development in Western Europe from 1750 to the present.* (London: Cambridge University Press, 1969).

THE VOLCANO IN THE COUNTRYSIDE

Ecomusée Creusot-Montceau, *Montceau-les-Mines: album 1856-2000* (Maçon: presses de l'Exprimeur, 2006).

D. La Chateau and N. De Centre, *La Representation du travail: Mines, forges, usines: [exposition] Chateau de la Verrerie, septembre 1977 - fevrier 1978.* (Le Creusot: Centre national de recherche d'animation et de création pour les arts plastiques - CRACAP Ecomusée de la Communaute Le Creusot-Montceau, 1977).

J. Antoine Roy, *Histoire de la famille Schneider et du Creusot* (Paris: M. Riviere, 1962).

M. Sutet and J. Pierre Bresillon, *Du terroir a l'usine: Le Creusot, Montceau-les-Mines autrefois.* (Le Coteau: Editions Horvath, 1983).

TRIUMPH AND SUFFERING

Arsène Bonafous-Murat, "Maurice Dumont, essai de catalogue de l'oeuvre gravé et lithographié." *Nouvelles de l'estampe* 6, no.115 (March/April 1991), 9-27.

Melissa Dabakis, *Visualizing Labor in American Sculpture: Monuments, manliness, and the work ethic, 1880-1935.* (Cambridge, U.K.: Cambridge University Press, 1999).

Eugenia W. Herbert, *The Artist and Social Reform: France and Belgium, 1885-1898* (New Haven: Yale University Press, 1961).

Robert L. Herbert and Eugenia W. Herbert, "Artists and Anarchism: Unpublished Letters of Pissarro, Signac and Others – I," *The Burlington Magazine*, 102, no. 692 (November 1960), 473-482.

Louis Lozowick, *Survivor From a Dead Age: the memoirs of Louis Lozowick.* Virginia Hagelstein Marquardt, ed. (Washington, D.C.: Smithsonian Institution Press, 1997).

Stéphane Michaud, Jean-Yves Mollier et Nicole Savy, eds. *Usages de l'image au XIXe siècle.* (Paris: Editions Créaphis, 1992).

I. Katherine Rigby, *An alle Kunstler: War – revolution – Weimar: German Expressionist prints, drawings, posters, and periodicals from the Robert Gore Rifkind Foundation* (San Diego, Calif.: San Diego State University Press, 1983).

Robyn Roslak, *Neo-Impressionism and Anarchism in Fin-de-Siecle France: Painting, politics and landscape* (Aldershot, England: Ashgate Pub, 2007).

Emile Verhaeren, *Œuvres* (Genève: Slatkine Reprints, 1977) 3 vols.

Barbara Wadsworth, *Edward Wadsworth: a painter's life* (Wilton, Salisbury: Michael Russell, 1989).

Checklist

The exhibition checklist is divided into eight sections, corresponding to different aspects of the progress of industry since the mid-eighteenth century. There is a brief note to each section describing its contents. Here are a few general notes on the format of individual entries.

When two or more artists have been involved in the creation of a print, the artist who designed the image is identified as "designer," whether the original design was a painting, a drawing, or in some other medium. The artist who prepared the printing plate or block itself is identified as "engraver."

Unless otherwise noted, dimensions given for a print are those of the composition, not including titles or other lettering unless they are an integral part of the image. Prints are measured to the nearest half-centimeter and the nearest eighth of an inch. Height precedes width.

When a print is identified as being "in" a book, the entire book is in the exhibition, open to the print in question. When it is described as being "from" a book or portfolio, the print is being shown by itself.

I. COALBROOKDALE

The little town of Coalbrookdale in the west of England was one of the cradles of the Industrial Revolution. In 1709 Abraham Darby introduced a new process there for smelting iron, using coke (coal that has been refined by heating in ovens) instead of charcoal. The business expanded under Darby's son and grandson.

Beginning with small items like pots and kettles, Darby's company graduated to cast-iron rails (for the horse-drawn railways used in and near coal mines) and cylinders for the first steam-engines (used to pump water out of the mines). A wagon carrying a giant cylinder appears in the foreground of *A View of the Upper Works at Coalbrook Dale* (no. 1). Abraham Darby III constructed the famous Coalbrookdale Iron Bridge (opened in 1780), the first major use of cast iron as a structural material (no. 4).

In the late eighteenth and early nineteenth century the industrial innovations at Coalbrookdale made it something of a tourist attraction. Numerous artists traveled there to depict the mines and ironworks.

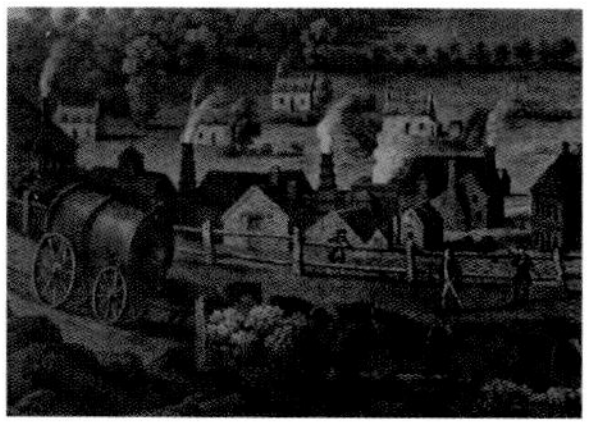

1. George Perry (designer), British, 1718 - 1771; and Thomas Smith of Derby (designer), British d. 1767
François Vivares (engraver), British, 1709 - 1780
A View of the Upper Works at Coalbrook Dale, 1758
engraving
36 x 52.5 cm (14 1/8 x 20 5/8 in.)

2. George Robertson (designer), British, 1746[9?] - 1788
Wilson Lowry (engraver), British, 1762 - 1824
An Iron Work for Casting of Cannon, and a Boring Mill, Taken from the Madeley Side of the River Severn, Shropshire, 1788
engraving
35 x 52.5 cm (13 3/4 x 20 5/8 in.)

3. George Robertson (designer), British, 1746[9?] - 1788
Francis Chesham (engraver), British, 1749 - 1806
A View of the Mouth of a Coal Pit near Broseley, in Shropshire, 1788
engraving
35.5 x 52 cm (14 x 20 1/2 in.)

4. George Robertson (designer), British, 1746[9?] - 1788
James Fittler (engraver), British, 1758 - 1835
A View of Lincoln Hill, with the Iron Bridge in the Distance Taken from the Side of the river Severn, 1788
engraving
35.5 x 52.5 cm (14 x 20 3/4 in.)

5. George Robertson (designer), British, 1746[9?] -1788
Wilson Lowry (engraver), British, 1762 - 1824
The Inside of a Smelting House at Broseley, Shropshire, 1788
engraving
35 x 52.5 cm (13 7/8 x 20 5/8 in.)

6. (fig. 1) Philip James de Loutherbourg (designer), British, 1740 - 1812
William Pickett (etcher), British, 1792 - 1820 *Iron Works, Colebrookdale*, 1805, from *The Romantic and Picturesque Scenery of England and Wales*
aquatint, hand-colored
25 x 32.5 cm (9 3/4 x 12 7/8 in.)

II. MINING

During the eighteenth and nineteenth centuries coal was the primary force in industrial development. In Britain, coal production rose from six million tons per year in 1770 to 220 million by 1900. Armies of miners fed the growing appetite of mills, railroads, and steamships for fuel. As late as the 1950s coal was the most important source of power for industry, and it continues to be one of the major fuels of the world today.

Coal mining was, and is, one of the most dangerous jobs in the world. Coal gives off gases that can asphyxiate miners, or explode. Water can flood the mine; a cave-in can kill miners or bury them alive. Part of the horror of a mine disaster is that it can take place miles below the surface. Friends and family may not know for days whether miners are still alive, and whether they can be rescued before food, water, or air run out. Two prints (nos. 17, 18), separated by almost two hundred years, present the same situation: the reaction above ground to an invisible catastrophe far below.

In art and literature coal miners have been presented as rough savages, as brave civilian soldiers providing the raw material of modern civilization, and as victims of the mine-owner's greed and indifference to safety.

7. (fig. 4) Thomas H. Hair, British, 1810 - 1882
Garesfield Colliery, 1839, in *The Mines of Durham and Northumbria*, 1844
etching
26.5 x 36.5 cm (10 3/8 x 14 1/2 in.) page size

8. Ignace François Bonhommé, French, 1809 - 1881
Coal Mines of Blanzy: The Lucie and Le Magny Group, 1857
lithograph in black and brown
49 x 66 cm (19 3/8 x 26 in.)

9. (fig. 9) Ignace François Bonhommé, French, 1809 - 1881
Montceau-les-Mines, 1857
lithograph in black and brown
36 x 99.5 cm. (14 1/4 x 39 1/4 in.)

10. Ignace François Bonhommé, French, 1809 - 1881
Coal Mines of Blanzy: the Montmaillot Mine Complex, 1857
lithograph in black and brown
42.5 x 66 cm (16 5/8 x 26 in.)

11. Joseph Pennell, American, 1875 - 1926
The Things that Tower: Collieries, 1909
etching
20 x 27.5 cm (7 7/8 x 10 7/8 in.)

12. (fig. 26) Elizabeth Olds, American, 1896 - 1991
"Bootleg" Mine, Pennsylvania, 1937
lithograph
25 x 35.5 cm (9 7/8 x 13 7/8 in.)

13. Maxime Dethomas, French, 1867 - 1929
National Loan: 1920, 1920
color lithograph
113.5 x 72.5 cm (44 1/2 x 28 5/8 in.)

14. Dessirier, French, twentieth century
Coal: Wealth of the Nation, 1958
lithograph in black and yellow
77.5 x 59.5 cm. (30 5/8 x 23 1/2 in.)

15. Maud and Miska Petersham, American, 1890 - 1971 and 1888 - 1960
Inside a Coal Mine, 1935, in *The Story Book of Coal*
color lithographs (picture book, published by John C. Winston 1935)
20.5 x 20 cm (8 x 7 7/8 in.) page size

16. German, twentieth century
Toy Coal Mine, 1950s?
color lithographs on steel
13.5 x 34.5 x 6.5 cm (5 3/8 x 13 1/2 x 2 3/8 in.)

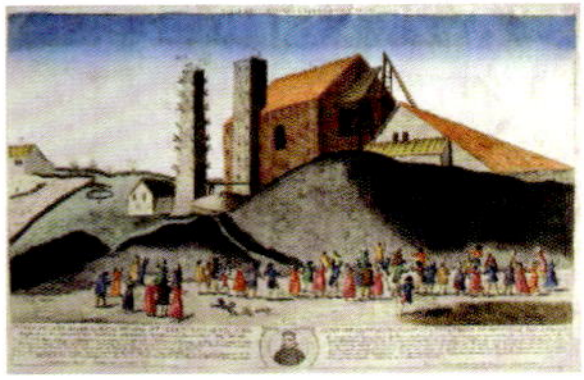

17. Unknown, French, nineteenth century
View of the Beaujonc Coal Mine near Liège, 1812
engraving, hand-colored
26 .5 x 43 cm (10 1/2 x 16 7/8 in.)

18. Raymond Mason, British, Born 1922
The Tragedy of Liévin, 1977
lithograph
32 x 39.5 cm (12 5/8 x 15 1/2 in.)

19. Maximilien Luce, French, 1858-1941
Leaving the Pits
lithograph
24.5 x 19 cm (9 5/8 x 7 1/2 in.)

20. Jules Gustave Besson (1868, active 1896-1925)
In the Black Country (Au Pays Noir), 1898, from *L'Estampe moderne*
color lithograph
36 x 24.5 cm (14 1/8 x 9 5/8 in.)

21. Eugène Carrière, French, 1849-1906
The Miner, 1900
lithograph in two tones of gray
119.5 x 80 cm (47 x 31 1/2 in.)

22. (fig. 21) Constantin Meunier, Belgian, 1831 - 1905
Miners, Borinage, 1898, from *Les Temps nouveaux*
lithograph
57.5 x 45.5 cm (22 5/8 x 17 7/8 in.)

23. (fig. 22) Gustave Pierre, French, 1875 - 1939
Miners at Rest, Underground, 1937, from *Charbonnages d'Hensies-Pommeroel*
etching
37 x 49.5 cm (14 1/2 x 19 1/2)

24. Gustave Pierre, French, 1875 - 1939
Miners Leaving Work, 1937, from *Charbonnages d'Hensies-Pommeroeul*
etching
36.5 x 49.5 cm (14 3/8 x 19 1/2 in.)

III. TRANSPORT AND CONSUMPTION

Mountains of coal traveled by barge or railroad car from the mines to large factories (nos 27, 28). Small workshops, too, depended on coal. In James McBey's etching of Venetian glass-blowers (no. 29), the heat to melt the glass may have come from a gas fire, but if so, the gas was coal-gas, made by heating coal in ovens. Natural gas did not begin to replace coal gas in Europe until the 1940s.

Today, coal consumption is much less visible than it was when coal trucks pulled up to the house with fuel for the furnace and the kitchen stove. When we think of cooking and heating, gas and electricity are the first things to come to mind. But much of the "clean" energy of electricity still comes from coal-fired generator plants like the one depicted by Louis Lozowick (no. 30).

The prints in this part of the exhibition show both commercial and domestic uses of coal: from the tons consumed by factories to the buckets of scrap coal picked up by scavengers (no. 32) to heat their own homes.

25. (fig. 12) Henri-Gabriel Ibels, French, 1867 - 1936
Theater Program: "The Weavers", 1892/3
color lithograph (proof before letters)
23 x 25 cm (9 x 9 3/4 in.)

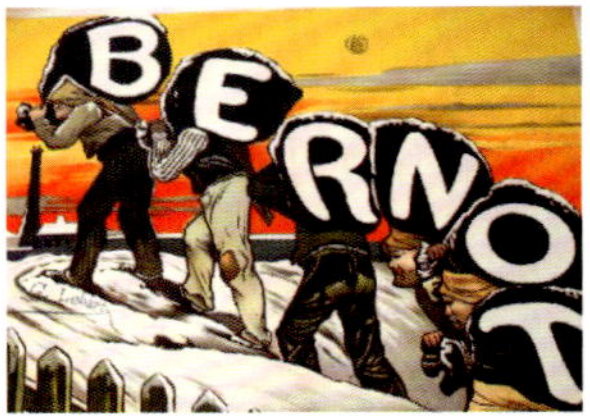

26. G. Lebart, French, active around 1900
Bernot Coal, 1895
color lithograph
56.5 x 75.5 cm. (22 1/4 x 29 3/4 in.)

27. Anonymous, French, around 1900
Factory View
color lithograph
29.5 x 46 cm (11 5/8 x 18 1/8 in.)

28. Roger Casse, French, 1880 - 1944
The Factory, circa 1930
color lithograph
45 x 51.5 cm (17 5/8 x 20 1/4 in.)

29. James McBey, British, 1893 - 1959
Glassblowers, Murano, 1925
drypoint
13 x 15 cm (5 1/8 x 6 in.)

30. (fig. 17) Louis Lozowick, American, 1892 - 1973
Edison Plant, 1929
lithograph
34.5 x 20 cm (13 5/8 x 7 7/8 in.)

31. Julius Tanzer, American, twentieth century
Harlem Coal Yard, 1936
lithograph
31 x 42 cm (12 1/8 x 16 5/8 in.)

32. (fig. 27) Robert Martin, American, 1888 - 1971
Coal Pickers, 1940
lithograph
25 x 20.5 cm (9 3/4 x 8 in.)

IV. IRON AND STEEL

Iron ore is one of the most abundant materials, and human beings have used it since ancient times. But before the 1750s iron and steel of high quality were scarce and expensive. Smelting (extracting iron from iron ore) and adding small amounts of other elements to give the iron or steel strength and flexibility were laborious processes with uncertain results. Producing good wrought iron or steel is like making a cake when the oven temperature is well over two thousand degrees, and the mixing bowl is in the oven!

In places like Coalbrookdale iron-smelters gradually developed processes that allowed them to make iron and steel in large quantities: enough for machinery, bridges, and skyscrapers. Two views of the French industrial center of Le Creusot show how between 1780 and 1870 it grew from a single ironworks to a vast complex for the production of iron and steel. Other prints in this section trace the progress of iron and steel from ore to finished product: furnaces that extract iron from the ore (nos. 35-38), a ladle pouring liquid iron or steel into molds (no. 39), the forging processes that shape the metals (nos. 40, 41), and the structures and machines that are made from them (nos. 43-46).

In several of the images we can see the transformation of industry that took place between 1850 and 1900, as machines, factories, and structures like bridges and ships grew bigger, and machine tools increasingly replaced handwork. In an engraving by James Sharples, for example, a team of workers hand-forges a piece of iron: George Clausen's later print shows a giant steam hammer for similar tasks.

33. (fig. 7) Anonymous, French, eighteenth century
View of the Foundry and Forges at Le Creusot, 1780s (printed after 1790)
etching
32 x 51 cm (12 1/2 in. x 20 in.)

34. André Gambey (designer), French, active 1873 - 1879
Le Creusot, 1873
photogravure from a painting
36.5 x 86 cm (14 3/8 x 33 7/8 in.)

35. (fig. 2) Thomas Allom (designer), British, 1804 - 1872
James Sands (engraver), British, 1811 - 1841
Lymington Iron Works on the Tyne, 1832, from *Durham and Northumberland Illustrated*
engraving, hand-colored
10 x 15.5 cm (3 7/8 x 6 1/8 in.)

36. Jean Joseph Bonaventure Laurens, French, 1801 - 1890
Blast Furnaces in Pouzin, 1871, from *Album du Chemin de Fer de Lyon à la Mediterranée. Cinquième Collection*
lithograph
14.5 x 24.5 cm (5 3/4 x 9 5/8 in.)

37. Maximilien Luce, French, 1858 - 1941
Blast Furnace, Factories at Charleroi, 1898, from *Pan*
color lithograph
35.5 x 27.5 cm (14 x 10 3/4 in.)

38. Harry Sternberg, American, 1904 - 2001
Blast Furnace #1, 1937
etching
30 x 22.5 cm (11 7/8 x 8 7/8 in.)

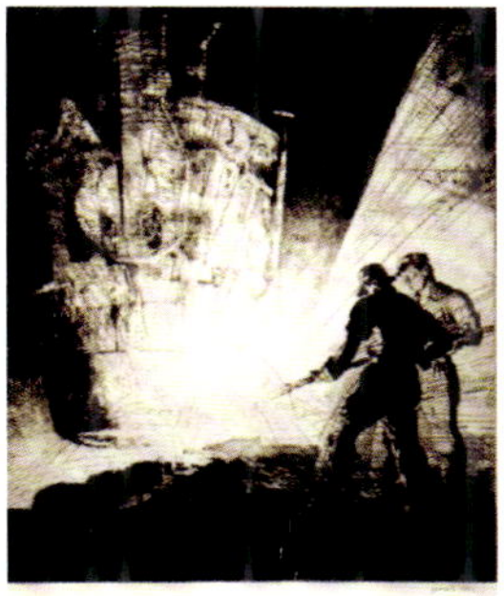

39. James E. Allen, American, 1894 - 1964
Teeming Ingots, 1935
etching
30 x 25 cm (11 7/8 x 9 7/8 in.)

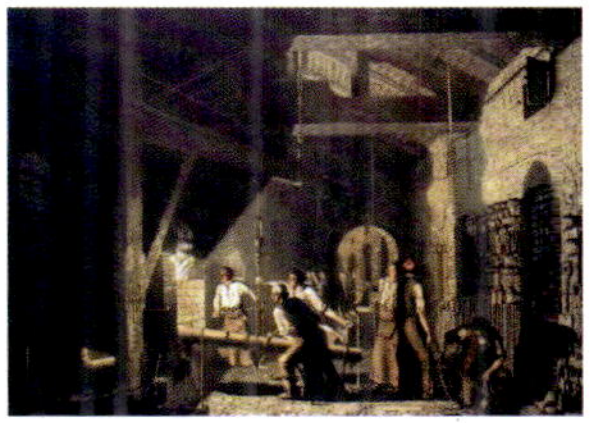

40. James Sharples, British, 1825 - 1893
The Forge, 1859
engraving, hand-colored
32.5 x 43 cm (12 7/8 x 17 in.)

41. George Clausen 1852 - 1944
The Great Hammer 1917, from *The Great War: Britain's Efforts and Ideals; Making Guns*
lithograph
35 x 45.5 cm (13 7/8 x 18 in.)

42. P. Grosjean, French, twentieth century
Fabrication of Bar Steel, 1930, in *Aciéries de Longwy*
photogravure in red and black
27 x 37 cm (10 5/8 x 13 5/8 in.)

43. (fig. 6) George Hawkins the younger, British, 1819 - 1852
Britannia Bridge, 1848
color lithograph
44.5 x 60.5 cm (17 1/2 x 23 3/4 in.)

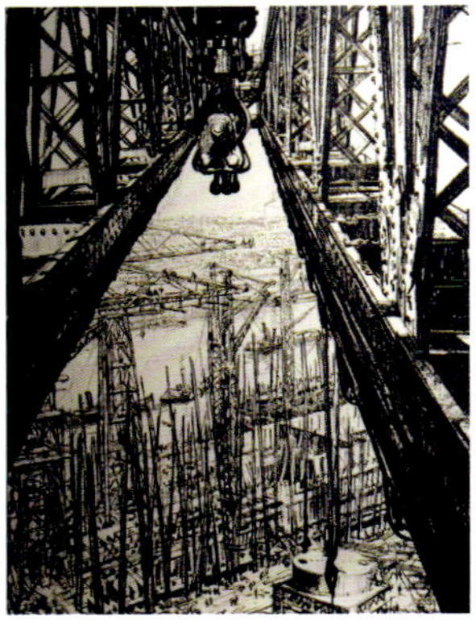

44. Muirhead Bone, British, 1876 - 1953
A Shipyard Seen from a Big Crane, circa 1917, from *The Great War: Britain's Efforts and Ideals; Building Ships*
lithograph
46.5 x 35.5 cm (18 1/4 x 14 1/8 in.)

45. (fig. 8) Emile Beaulieu, American, active 1852 - 1865
Bridesburg Machine Works, 1856
color lithograph
47.5 x 76 cm (18 5/8 x 29 7/8 in.)

46. Tamagno, French, twentieth century
Peugeot, circa 1920
color lithograph
150 x 111 cm (59 1/4 x 43 5/8 in.)

V. GAS LIGHT AND STEAM POWER

Refining coal into coke for iron-smelting gave rise to a by-product: the gas that was produced when the coal was baked in ovens. Coal-gas soon found its own uses as a fuel and a source of light. It provided the best available lighting for streets, houses, and factories all through the nineteenth century. The first internal-combustion engines, like the Crossley engine shown on a calendar for the Pierson gas company, were designed to run on coal-gas.

Long before the gas engine, the coal-iron-steam triad revolutionized transportation. For centuries roads made with wooden or metal rails, and wagons built to run on them, had carried coal out of the mine or from the mine to a river or canal. In 1804, a steam engine first replaced horses on one of these "rail-ways" and over the next century railways spread across the world. The advance in railroad engines can be measured by comparing Bourne's print of the first railroad out of London (no. 53) and Kasimir's of a giant German locomotive about a hundred years later (no. 54).

Steam also powered boats, cranes like those in the prints by Raleigh and Detwiller, and machinery of all kinds. In the typical nineteenth-century factory a large steam engine transmitted power to individual machine tools through an elaborate system of spinning drums and belts. Nevinson's view of an aircraft engine factory during the First World War (no. 55) shows how the system worked. By Nevinson's time it would soon be obsolete, as smaller gas or electric motors replaced the large central steam engine as a power source in factories.

47. (fig. 3) William Read, British, active 1820 - 1839
Drawing the Retorts, Brick Lane Gas Works, 1821, in Colin MacKenzie: *A Thousand Experiments in Chemistry*
aquatint, hand colored
16.5 x 22.5 cm (6 1/2 x 8 7/8 in.)

48. Gustave Doré, French, 1832 - 1882/3
Lambeth Gas Works, 1872, from *London, a Pilgrimage*
wood engraving
25 x 19.5 cm (9 3/4 x 7 5/8 in.)

49. (fig. 19) Compagnie Française des papiers-monnaie, French, active 1890s
J. and O. G. Pierson, Calendar for 1896, 1895
engraving
15 x 20.5 cm (6 x 8 in.)

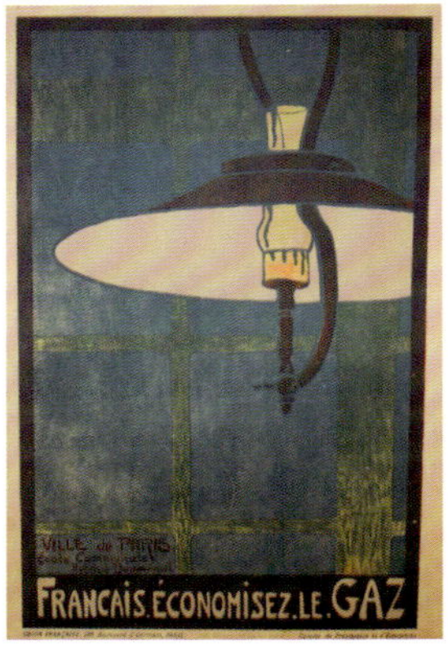

50. Anonymous, French, early twentieth century
Economize on Gaslight, 1917
color lithograph
49.5 x 31.5 cm (19 1/2 x 12 1/2 in.)

51. Hermann Raunheim (designer), German, worked in France, 1817 - 1895
Aumont and Leroux (H. Aumont and Alexandre Leroux) (lithographers), French, active 1849 - 1867
National Rubber Company, Langlée Factory, 1850s
lithograph
23.5 x 39.5 cm (9 1/4 x 5 5/8 in.)

52. Henry Raleigh, American, 1880 - 1946
Bridgeport Barges
etching
24 x 38 cm (9 1/2 x 15 in.)

53. (fig. 5) John Cooke Bourne, British, 1814 - 1896
Berkhampstead, Herts. June 10th 1837, in *Drawings of the London and Birmingham Railway*, 1839
lithograph in black and gray
25.5 x 38.5 cm (10 1/8 x 15 1/8 in.)

54. Luigi Kasimir, Austrian, 1881 - 1962
Henschel Locomotive, South Africa, circa 1953
etching and aquatint, printed in color
65.5 x 53 cm (25 7/8 x 20 7/8 in.)

55. (fig. 23) C. R. W. Nevinson, British, 1889 - 1946
Making the Engine, 1917, from *The Great War: Britains Efforts and Ideals; Building Aircraft*
lithograph
40.5 x 30 cm (15 7/8 x 11 7/8 in.)

56. (fig. 16) Frederick K. Detwiller, American, 1882 - 1953
The Spur, New York City, 1924
lithograph
52 x 35.5 cm (20 3/8 x 14 in.)

VI. THE SMOKESTACK LANDSCAPE

The tall chimney does two things: it increases the flow of air to the fire (and the heat the fire generates) and it helps carry away smoke and its pollutants. Wherever coal was burned in large quantities – to smelt iron, to work steel, or to power steam machinery – a smokestack was there. The more industry grew, the taller and more numerous the smokestacks became.

For about two centuries the tall stack with its plume of smoke has been an ambivalent image: a symbol of both prosperity and pollution. An artist can manipulate an image to emphasize one message or the other. Where isolated plumes of smoke punctuate a blue sky we are more inclined to think of active industry, full employment, and its profit. When the smoke plumes blend and cover the sky, we think of a poisoned environment.

57. Henry Warren (designer), British, 1793 - 1879
George Greatbach (engraver), British, active 1850 - 1869
The Black Country (near Bilston)
engraving, hand-colored
14 x 19 cm (5 1/2 x 7 1/2 in.)

58. (fig. 10) Camille Pissarro, French, 1831 - 1903
Factory at Pontoise, 1874
etching
12.5 x 8.5 cm (4 7/8 x 3 1/4 in.)

59. (fig. 15) Joseph Pennell, American, 1857 - 1926
The Great Stack, Sheffield, 1909
etching
32 x 24 cm (12 1/2 x 9 1/2 in.)

60. (fig. 24) Henri Baptiste Lebasque, French, 1865 - 1937
Peace Loan (Emprunt de la Paix), 1918
color lithograph
108.5 x 76 cm (42.3/4 x 29 7/8 in.)

61. (fig. 25) Cesar Klein, German, 1876 - 1954
The One Who Does not Work is his Children's Gravedigger (Wer nicht Arbeitet is der Totengräber seiner Kinder), 1919
color lithograph
115 x 79.5 cm. (45 1/2 x 31 1/4 in.)

62. E. M. Ashe, American, 1867 - 1941
After the Welcome Home, a Job, 1919
color lithograph
105 x 71 cm (41 3/8 x 28 in.)

63. (fig. 13) Jean Émile Laboureur, French, 1877 - 1943
The Factories, 1902
etching
12.5 x 18 cm (5 x 7 in.)

64. (fig. 11) Maximilien Luce, French, 1858 - 1941
Rotterdam Harbor, circa 1908
etching
29.5 x 38.5 cm (11 5/8 x 15 1/4 in.)

65. Herbert Lespinasse, American, worked in France, 1884 - 1972
Factories, 1914-16
woodcut
22.5 x 29.5 cm (8 7/8 x 11 5/8 in.)

VII. LIFE AND LABOR

Over the last two centuries human beings have accommodated themselves – sometimes willingly, sometimes grudgingly – to the changed world brought about by the Industrial Revolution. This part of the exhibition shows documentary and symbolic responses to life in that world.

Romance flowers among miners and factory workers in posters for a novel, *The Black-Faces*, and a lost silent film, *The Black Wall*. Prints by Wadsworth and Kreienbuhl (nos. 70, 72) depict domestic life in the shadow of industry. In a tiny print by Maurice Dumont (no. 67), female figures suggest a spiritual presence in the industrial environment, and Pascale Hémery's *Woman-Factory* (no. 73) is a symbolic evocation of the growing power of women in architecture and industrial design in the 1920s and 1930s. Finally, Steinlen's *The Last Refuge of Liberty* (no. 66) and Sternberg's *Enough* (no. 71) link politics and labor.

66. (fig. 20) Théophile Steinlen, Swiss, 1859 - 1923
The Last Refuge of Liberty, 1894
lithograph
33.5 x 27.5 (13 1/8 in. x 10 7/8 in.)

67. (fig. 14) Maurice Dumont, French, 1870 - 1899
Untitled, 1895, plate 4 from *Surroundings of the City* (Autour de la ville)
drypoint and aquatint
11.5 x 8 cm (4 5/8 x 3 1/8 in.)

68. Théophile Steinlen, Swiss, 1859 - 1923
The Black-Faces, (Les gueules noires), 1907
lithograph in black and brown
42.5 x 55 cm (16 3/4 x 21 3/4 in.)

69. Vitagraph company (publisher), American, 1897 - 1925
The Black Wall, 1910
color lithograph
129.5 x 89.5 cm (51 1/8 x 35 1/8 in.)

70. (fig. 18) Edward Wadsworth, British, 1889 - 1949
Yorkshire, 1920
woodcut
11.5 x 15 cm (4 1.2 x 6 in.)

71. Harry Sternberg, American, 1904 - 2001
Enough, 1947
aquatint
38 x 30 cm (14 7/8 x 11 3/4 in.)

72. Jürg Kreienbühl, Swiss, born 1932
The Campground of the Poor, 1981
lithograph
43 x 69 cm (17 x 27 1/4 in.)

73. Pascale Hémery, French, born 1965
Woman-Factory (La Femme-Usine), 1998
color linocut
30 x 21.5 cm (11 7/8 x 8 3/8 in.)

VIII. EPILOGUE

In the last fifty years the worldwide industrial landscape has changed drastically. Coal mining has ceased in Europe. China now produces five times as much steel as the United States. With coal, oil, and nuclear power challenged by advocates of natural sources like sun, wind, and tide, the future of energy is likely to be much more diverse, and more diffuse, in the coming century than it was in the last two. As we tear down obsolete mine and factory buildings or turn them into museums of industrial history, artists have begun to look at them with the nostalgic awe that ruined temples or castles have evoked in the past.

Each of the three artists represented in this section has taken a different approach to the transformation of the industrial world. Trignac's *Refinery* (no. 75) is a fantasy, showing a steel forest engulfed by a natural one. Secheret's view of a cliff-like building (no. 74) is the memorial to a steel plant that was closing down at the time he depicted it and has since been demolished.

In contrast, McPherson's *Clairton* (no. 76) shows a still-active plant for producing coke, the form of coal that is essential for production of iron and steel, just as it was in Coalbrookdale two hundred and fifty years ago. The combination of night, fire, and smoke is as dramatic today as it was in early views of industry. But as our hopes for the future center on clear skies and clean energy, McPherson's image has the fascination of a look into the past.

74. (fig. 29) Jean-Baptiste Secheret, French, born 1957
Mondeville, 1991
color monotype
69.5 x 88.5 cm. (27 1/4 x 34 7/8 in.)

75. Gérard Trignac, French, born 1955
The Refinery, 1993
etching, engraving and drypoint
45 x 39-43 cm (17 5/8 x 15 3/8-16 7/8 in.)

76. (fig.28) Craig McPherson, American, born 1948
Clairton, 1997
mezzotint on green paper
35 x 42 cm (13 7/8 x 16 5/8 in.)